"*Please Talk about Me When I'm Gone*, which pulled me in from the first page and never let go, is a mosaic love letter from a son to his lost mother, so everyone in the bereavement club should read it. But this memoir is also a thoughtful, compassionate meditation on being alive. I nodded in recognition, dog-eared pages containing lines I loved, felt my eyes well with tears. In the end you should read it for the reason anyone reads good writing: to feel less alone."

—JENNA BLUM, *New York Times* bestselling author of *Those Who Save Us* and *The Stormchasers*

"As an oncologist treating a difficult and often fatal group of cancers, I witness firsthand as patients and their 'villages' cope with the diagnosis. So many decisions, so much emotion, and everyone does it a bit differently. No one path will serve; instead it is a truly individual course we choose. Sean Murphy's book is a great new resource for patients and families, and frankly for us all."

—DR. JOHN MARSHALL, Chief of Oncology,
Georgetown University Hospital

"In some moments of profound experience, we see and feel in extraordinary ways. That is what happened to Sean Murphy after his mother's death. He has had the courage to look honestly at death, and the talent to express his love and grief in a way that will comfort and sustain his readers."

—STEPHEN GOODWIN, author of
Breaking Her Fall and *Dream Golf*

"Sean Murphy brings a poetic voice and insightful contemplations to the largely unexplored territory of dying and death. With deep compassion and philosophical curiosity, he processes his individual grief while confirming the universality of loss."

—ROY REMER, Director of Volunteer Programs,
Zen Hospice Project

"An extremely moving, beautifully written, heartfelt and touching chronicling of the life and death of a parent."

—CHARLES SALZBERG, author of
Devil in the Hole and *Swann Dives In*

"As both the President of a colorectal cancer nonprofit, and more importantly a son who also lost his mother to this disease, I found this memoir at once emotional, educational, and edgy. I highly recommend this read for patients, survivors, caretakers, and physicians alike. An amazing story—Sean Murphy's mother would be proud."

—MICHAEL SAPIENZA, President and Founder,
Chris4Life Colon Cancer Foundation

"Sean Murphy writes of his loss in a way that is compelling and insightful. Anyone early in the process of grief should hear his message—that you never get over the death of a loved one, and that's as it should be."

—ELIZABETH ROGERS, Social Worker,
Advanced Illness Management Program

"When I started *Please Talk about Me When I'm Gone*, I read a section and said to myself, 'I'm going to email Sean to tell him how amazing that sentence is.' Then as I read a little further I thought, 'No, I'm going to email Sean to tell him what an amazing depth of knowledge and perception he's giving us.' And then, yes, you got it, on the very next page he wrote something that made me think, 'His mom is looking down on Sean with unending love for what he just wrote.' This is one amazing book!"

—DONALD R. GALLEHR, Director Emeritus,
Northern Virginia Writing Project

Please Talk about Me When I'm Gone

Please Talk about Me When I'm Gone

A Memoir for My Mother

SEAN MURPHY

BRIGHT
MOMENTS
BOOKS

BRIGHT MOMENTS BOOKS
Reston, Virginia
Printed in the United States of America

Library of Congress Control Number: 2013915366

Please Talk about Me When I'm Gone: a memoir for my
mother / Sean Murphy

ISBN 978-0-989-88050-3

The author gratefully acknowledges permission to use the following:
Excerpts from "On Angels" and "Return to Kraków in 1880"
by Czeslaw Milosz, from *The Collected Poems*, Ecco Publishing,
copyright © 1990 by Czeslaw Milosz. Excerpts from "Those Winter
Sundays" by Robert Hayden, from *Collected Poems*, Liveright
Publishing, copyright © 1997 by Robert Hayden.

Book design and typesetting by Anton Khodakovsky
Author photograph page 287 courtesy of Paul Misencik
All other photographs courtesy of the author

Visit the author's website at
SEANMURPHY.NET

For Linda Murphy,

my mother, my first teacher, and my first friend,
the woman who brought me into this world
and allowed me to help her leave it

I have heard that voice many a time when asleep
and, what is strange, I understood more or less
an order or an appeal in an unearthly tongue:

day draws near
another one
do what you can.

—Czeslaw Milosz

Prologue: Encomium

AUGUST 30, 2002. I thought: *Everything that is good about me is because of my mother.*

I was in a church for the first time in forever. The church where I served its first-ever mass as an altar boy. The church where I received the Sacrament of Confirmation. The church where my parents celebrated their twenty-fifth wedding anniversary. The church where my sister got married. The church where I almost got married.

My father had said: *Obviously you'll deliver the eulogy.*

Question: How will I get through it?

How did you get through it, friends and family asked.

Answer: I don't know.

Everyone who cares about my mother, or cares about one of us who loves her, has had a certain heaviness in their hearts these past five years, as she has bravely battled this illness that ultimately claimed her body—only to ensure that her spirit could survive, like a million small fires inside of all our hearts.

It had been half a lifetime since I'd experienced this vantage point. Standing on the altar, looking down at a church filled with somber, expectant faces. All those years as an altar boy, hearing the words and receiving the ritual on its austere terms, the practiced movements and mannerisms that sought to convey the meaning—and purpose—of existence in sixty minutes or less. Carefully studying the priest who presided over the congregation, routinely looking up at those stained glass images that looked down at us, filling the room with an inexpressible piety and approbation.

Periodically I would be called on to serve a wedding and less frequently a funeral. Weddings were preferable for both obvious and selfish reasons: happy events, pretty women, and typically a few extra dollars for my time. The funerals were, in practically

every sense, the opposite. I'd only been to one funeral before becoming an altar boy, and while I'd been old enough, at ten, to remember it, I mostly recalled how surreal it was to see my grandmother in an open casket, and the way my mother, her siblings, and their father wept; not being able to console them or fully grasp the depth of my own sorrow.

"Listen to the words," my father had told me, sensing my ambivalence before I prepared, at age twelve, for my first funeral mass. "It's actually a very beautiful service." I listened to him, and I listened to the words. I listened to everything, then. The passages and prayers—some familiar, some not—were carefully chosen, and went a considerable way toward impressing upon my adolescent mind how communal, and inevitable, this rite of passage was for everyone who drew breath. Someday each of us will watch a loved one die, and eventually all of us will pass on from *here* to *there.* That's where the meaning of the words—and whether or not you believed them—came into play. I believed the words; I believed everything, then.

The time was World War II, and like so many others of her remarkable generation, the baby girl her parents named Linda came into the world while her father was half a world away, honorably doing his duty for the country his own father had only recently learned to call home.

The first of seven siblings, she became in many regards a mother long before giving birth, a preparation that would serve her well when she became a young mother, suddenly several thousand miles from the family she lived with and then left, along with her husband, having the courage and conviction to make their way and create a life of their own.

She said: *I'll never leave you.*

Neither of us realized, then, that in addition to comforting me—like she always did—she was also preparing me for this moment.

She knew what it was like to leave. *How,* she must have wondered, *did I end up here?* First in the dry expanse of Arizona, and later just outside the nation's capital, while the rest of her family—brothers and sisters and all those nieces, nephews, brothers-in-law and sisters-in-law—remained just outside Boston. All the questions she learned not to ask. Or, rather, she came to realize there are no good answers for. And more, if we're lucky in life, we don't need to ask after a while.

The reason I can confidently proclaim my mother is still around is because of the obsessions that infuse my identity: the passion for art and expression, the advocacy of justice and tolerance, the unending pursuit of honesty and compassion. These are inexorable imprints; they are, in fact, the essence of my mother, and her soul is in my soul, as it always has been, as it always will be.

Looking out, all my familiar faces: my father, my sister, her husband, my nephew and niece, the two aunts—my mother's sisters—who had been with us for those awful, awe-inspiring final two weeks, and behind them the confidantes, colleagues, childhood friends, grown-up acquaintances, friends' parents, and all the less recognizable faces I hadn't seen in so many years. This is the closest we come to witnessing our own funerals. The same people there to support us, smile and cry with us, becoming part of the moments that become memories; an event that connects us and brings us closer, no matter how far away or disparate our lives might otherwise be.

Looking out at my family and understanding that they helped shape me, that I wouldn't change anything even if I could. We learn to put away childish things and earn the chances we've been given, the responsibility to carry on the work that has already been done on our behalf. Equal parts fate and good fortune, we look at those familiar faces and understand what they have done, and what we need to do.

What will I remember? I'll remember everything. The things I've expressed and the things I saw, the things I still see in the eyes and actions of those around me. I will remember her as my first teacher and first friend, the woman who brought me into the world and allowed me to help her leave it. I will remember that soft, sweet silence, just like she had gone to sleep. Only more.

I think: *Everything that is good about me is because of my mother.*

Alive

(2002)

IT ALWAYS WAITS until after you're asleep.

(You think: *Who are you?*)

(And then you remember.)

Memories. Not the unyielding, excruciating moments near or at the end, but the better times. Or even worse, the arbitrary moments in life that dug in deep, long before the mind has discarded them.

In the dark, afraid to close my eyes now, afraid of the not-quite-nothingness that awaits me there. Like a boy, again. Afraid of the dark; afraid to close my eyes.

Too much like death?

No. It was too much like *life*.

Sleep and death both prolonged peacefulness. The quiet, uncomplicated ability to forget suffering and self. Awake (*I think, therefore I am*, I think).

What are you doing?

I can't find an explanation for how I came to be here, but there has to be a story. There's always a story.

(There's a dark space between what we can tell others and what we'll only tell ourselves, and that is Truth. And there's a darker space that contains the things we can't even tell ourselves; those things speak their own language—in dreams, memories, and mistakes—so we try to make sense of it any way we can, and that is Art.)

Here's the story: Everything had played out pretty much according to everyone's expectations. It all more or less happened the way I'd envisioned it would. And I'd had plenty of time (all that anxious time, all those empty hours) to imagine how it would unwind, which was not necessarily the way I might have foreseen it, beforehand. Before it all began.

After the long wait and eventual end of it, there was the *afterward*, that first day of the rest of our lives.

We did it, I thought. We made it.

At least, I thought, the hard part is over.

No. I knew, even then, that this wasn't true. It was too soon to say that.

Okay. At least the *worst* part was behind us. It had taken five years: from first surgery until the day after, almost exactly five years. It had taken more than any of us could give. It had taken more than any of us could bear to give up. Now (I hoped), all we had to do was somehow go about the business of living. Just live our lives, I thought.

The worst (I knew), was over.

No, that's not the truth.

The worst was only beginning?

No, not that either.

Only this: We had the rest of our lives to live.

Please Talk about Me When I'm Gone

(2013)

L'AMOUR DE L'ART fait perdre l'amour vrai.

I didn't say that.

Although that's the sort of thing I might say, since I'm the sort who feels obliged to quote the books I've read and I allow art to remind me how to relate to myself.

The love of art means loss of real love.

Some people, sometimes, choose to make their lives more complicated. Life, sometimes, decides for them; sometimes life gets there first.

To win? To lose?

What for, if the world will forget us anyway.

I didn't write that. A *poet* wrote that. I'm no poet. Poets are always looking for things, such as heroes. Who wants to be a hero these days? Who can afford it? The world could be—and might very well already be—full of folks who will ring changes and do their part to shake up the constricting and crazed institutions that keep us chained, bound and complacent. There are lots of these people, I'm sure: tons and tons of them. But the thing is, most of us are too busy trying to live. It's enough just to survive without seeking to pursue such lofty, such *poetic* propositions.

This is the new poetry: the more things stay the same, the more they change. Here is our art: haikus of horror in the cities, sonnets of sin and corruption, limericks of deregulation, free verse free trade, rhymed lines of laissez-faire, and the emboldened ghost writer, Death, forever at work on our collective life stories.

These days we look for poetry in all the wrong places. Some of us even believe we're gazing more deeply into the murky waters of existence when all we're actually seeing is our own reflections.

And so (I think): A life is not unlike a poem, too often eager to please, predictable, safe. I think: One should, therefore, feel obliged occasionally to ask some complicated questions. Such as: What am I doing to keep things interesting? What can I do to generate momentum, keep the narrative flowing?

Listen: When some of your best friends are people who exist *elsewhere*—characters in books you've read, musicians you'll never meet, people from the past who died decades (even centuries) before you were born, or people you knew intimately who are no longer around—it might be time to ask some complicated questions.

Who are you?

That is, or should be, the first question, as well as the last question, and it should be asked as often as possible along the way.

You see, all men *are* islands. After all, no one else is inside you when you're born, no one is going with you when you die, and between those first and last breaths, the decisions, actions, and accountability are your own. All, all yours.

So: You find friends, you seek solace in yourself, you learn to discern redemption through the aimless affairs that comprise the push and pull of everyone's existence. You realize, in short, that you're going through it alone, so you should never go through it *alone*. You can't run away, and the farther you run, the closer you get to yourself. And you're all you've got.

If you're fortunate enough to figure this out early on, you find friends: the real ones who exist in your everyday world, and the *other* ones who have been there all along, the ones you can always turn to, wherever or whoever you happen to be.

Please talk about me when I'm gone. That's the title of this memoir. It's also the presumptive title of any memoir. More, it's the unwritten title of any work of art—a desire to have those thoughts and feelings articulated, read, understood, appreciated. More still, it's the often unexpressed message of any individual life: We want to be discussed, loved, and celebrated after we're no longer around. Mostly we don't want to be quickly or easily forgotten.

When you hear voices, or find yourself talking to people you're not sure can hear you, you should cut yourself some slack. We've all been there—or will be at some point. We've all, on occasion, looked up to the clouds and wondered if there was a kingdom beyond the skies, the place some of us were told our dearly departed looked down from. Haven't we all taken comfort from a one-way conversation we forgot to be self-conscious about? Aren't we all, at times, unable or unwilling to entirely abandon the idea that someone else is listening?

And so: You talk. And maybe, someone listens. Anyone might be listening up there, and that's more comfort than anything you could ever find in a church. And so: You talk. Say something, everything. Say anything you need to say to survive.

Who knows but that, on the lower frequencies, I speak for you?
What he said.

Calculus

(2013)

MY GRIEF HAS made me, against all previous likelihood, into a half-assed mathematician. Numbers were never my bag, and I've got the report cards to prove it. And yet, ever since 2002, I find myself going over similar calculations, repeatedly.

There are the obvious, inevitable examples. For instance, on August 26, 2004: This is the *second* anniversary of her death; it is therefore *seven* years since her first operation. Then, with a combination of improvisation and OCD, other variations ensue: I was twenty-seven at that first operation; my nephew will be twenty-seven when I'm fifty-seven, which is two years younger than my mother was when she died. My mother's funeral cost about (insert dollar amount here), which would buy (this many) trips to (this place). If we went to the various hospitals and treatment centers approximately fifty times over the course of five years, at roughly fifteen miles per trip, this distance would get you from D.C. to Chicago. We ate in the hospital cafeteria roughly twenty times, or enough to pay 2 percent of one of the cashier's yearly salary. And so on.

And then this, revisited on a regular basis: If I get diagnosed at fifty-four, like my mother did, that means that effective immediately I have x years and y months to enjoy a cancer-free existence (although those malevolent cells could be coursing through my oblivious veins even as I type). Interestingly, the likes of this last equation—and the scenarios it induces—seldom extend to my old man or my sister. It is, I reckon, disconcerting enough to apply these exercises to myself; it is intolerable (or, at least for now, not possible) to project them onto anyone else.

I can barely balance my checkbook, yet here I am, a poor-man's Pythagoras, my busy brain co-opting or pre-empting the confusion and consternation cancer yields. And just like the bad old days during Algebra exams, I apprehend much less than I'd like. For example: How might my mother have lived her life if she'd known she was never going to see sixty? How might *I* have lived? How might I do things differently (i.e., *better*) if I could know how far off, or how unacceptably close my own death will be?

Once again, it gets back to God, the Prime Mover with an advanced degree in these metaphysical matters. Or at least it prompts a concession to—or yearning for—some immutable force that organizes, if not explains, the mystery of being, as well as the when's, what's, and why's of how we come and where we go.

But every dog has its day, right? Take my dog, for good measure. I knew he was going to die (he died when I was thirty-eight, which was six years after my mother died…). I know *I'm* going to die. My friends' children will die. Puppies and kids not even born will have litters and grandchildren who will one day die, and it's not easy to predict which ones may go before their time because none of us knows how long we've got once we get here.

And up there, somewhere, that benevolent, or oblivious, or nonexistent—depending on which courses you've taken in life—entity is crunching the numbers and checking His work, using the magic red pen to cross out errors or correct any formulas that are inconsistent with the bigger picture, which itself is an open book, and always a work in progress.

In the Air (1)

(1996)

THIS STORY BEGINS with a plane flight.

Or, it begins with what a son feared, watching a man who could have been his father on that flight. He envisioned his father dying first, on a plane. Which made him think about his mother, who had not at that time felt those initial pains that would require the first surgery. Six years later, after he and his father and his sister found themselves still alive, he would remember the plane flight, and what it had told him about his father, his mother, and himself. And maybe how that story should have been about his mother, after all: about the fears and premonitions she could never quell, having seen her own mother die too young, also of cancer (brain vs. colon, the head vs. the gut, different, the same). In a time—not all that long ago—when they didn't tell you how much time you could expect, because everyone knew what to expect: the worst. And after, the grief while preparing for her own *inevitable*, whether it was the same sort of sickness or the more mundane handiwork of old age and infirmity. Her son saw all this, and how, he would think, could this not color his consciousness? Was he already fated to think the way his mother did? Was he already dying inside of the disease she didn't yet detect?

Maybe the story begins before any of this. Or after it all; always thinking about what had not even happened, in some undetermined, unknowable future.

Perhaps this story begins with the stories: the ways he experienced things and how his imagination would render them—in memories, daydreams, and especially stories. Seeing the world; seeing his life; seeing the stories through other sets of eyes; immortalizing incidents that never actually happened—all in an effort to avoid being forgotten. (*Please remember me when I'm gone.*) In order to remember any of it there needs to be a story, and every story needs to begin someplace. So, for this story, let it begin with a young man who is actually me, sitting on a plane, watching a man who could have been his father—in another life, in a different story—and contemplating what had happened and what was going to happen.

Old School
(1977)

You've come a long way kid, I do not say to myself.

You can't go home again, the saying goes. Of course, if you never leave, you're already there. But you still think about things. Today, I can walk past the school that seemed like a skyscraper, circa 1977. That's the comfort of cliché, and I wear it when I need to, when I can. My hometown—Reston, Virginia—grew up. I grew up. Today, I look in at a classroom I may have sat in during a different century, a different lifetime. I see myself reflected in that window and wonder if I ever could have envisioned seeing this man on the outside, looking in.

You *have* come a long way, if you think about it (I think).

Think about it: Remember first grade? I was *that* kid, the pitiful little chump crying for his mother on the first day of school (the first day of the rest of your life, you did not think). It was inexplicable, even to me, on some levels. After all, kindergarten had been a cakewalk: all year, not a single issue, certainly no separation anxiety. So what happened? Stage fright stepping into the big leagues? Latent mama's-boy syndrome? The birth of an anxiety that would stalk me like the weak and injured prey I sometimes was, on and off throughout childhood? All of the above?

16

The teacher, as I recall, was as sympathetic as she could be, but the show had to go on. This was old school, which is not to say it was *old* school: a generation or two earlier and the teacher probably would have paddled my ass and I would have been singled out, then and there, as *that* kid. I *was* that kid, but I got over it. Most kids do.

My poor mother. As if she wasn't having her own problems, watching her second-born child (the *baby*) go from half-days to full days (the novelty of lunch; the redemption of recess), walking there and back, over a mile each way (this was old school, after all) and taking that next step away from her embrace and into the open if hostile arms of the wicked, wonderful world. Why was her son having issues where her daughter had none? She did what any reasonable mother would do: she figured maybe I wasn't ready, or that I needed a little more encouragement, or that maybe if we all wished intently enough we could suspend time and it would stay 1977 forever. All of which is to say, it was intolerable to her as a mother and as a woman—as a sensitive human being—to imagine her son melting down once she was out of his sight.

Fortunately for all of us, sterner heads prevailed. Pops would have none of it (he was old school), and he stepped in and assumed the role of bad cop, the role every father eventually embraces with varying degrees of ambivalence. After all, their kids aren't going to police themselves, are they? Before they can learn the Golden Rule, they have to understand what rules are. (This hurts me more than it hurts you, they don't say.) And above all, you can't stand by and do nothing while your son turns into a sissy before your eyes.

"That was a tough one," he would later say (he'll say it now if you ask him). "But I knew, if we didn't make you go to school, we knew…"

He never really finishes that thought and he never really has to. We all know what that would, or could have led to. For me; for anyone. And I'm not talking about ludicrous clichés like becoming a sissy (are sissies born or made?) or crawling back into the womb—metaphorically speaking. Sometimes it's enough just to be *that* kid.

I remember him taking me to school that second (and maybe third) day, grimacing at me once the waterworks started and asking me if I wanted him to take off his belt (he was old school). I didn't want him to take off his belt, and I didn't want to go into that classroom: my first quandary, a real-time cause and effect not found in a coloring book. The chess game was on and I could barely play checkers, but even a seven-year-old knows when it's his move. Ultimately the fear of the belt prevailed (perhaps, on some subconscious level, the anathema of becoming *that* kid also played a part). Old School kicked New Age's ass, and all was right in the world and the Gospel According to Pops.

The story has a happy ending, but it doesn't end there.

In the interest of full disclosure, while I was able (or obliged) to make the lonely march into that classroom, I still needed a little time to complete this transition. I'm not sure how it happened, but for at least a day and possibly as long as a week, I latched on to some unfortunate second grader. Naturally, at that age—and all through high school—it's remarkable how the kids only one year older might as well be an entirely different species. This particular kid (who, in the interest of fullest disclosure, I seem to recall was named David, but that's a leap of faith giving my memory more credit than it deserves) was taller, quiet, and—I must have instinctively understood—an alpha dog.

I followed him around like a puppy, and even as I could sense he was appalled by my desperation, I took considerable solace in the fact that he didn't deny me. In fact, my simile is apt, because I recall he tolerated me much like an older dog deals with a sharp-toothed and impertinent pup: that look of wary exasperation, the resigned acknowledgment that it can't cast out one of its own kind. Between Pop's belt and David's benevolence, I found the necessary ingredients—and impetus—for advancement: I was on my way.

A quick shout out to David, wherever you may be (and whatever your name actually is): I thank you for letting me cling to you like a remora as we cruised the halls and cubbies I would soon become comfortable with. Perhaps your example gave me an early appreciation for underdogs and those amongst us who just need a little encouragement, a little solidarity. I hope, if you have kids, they are well-adjusted and independent and have a healthy dose of old school. And if they aren't, I hope they seek out a second grader as patient as you were, back in another lifetime when you unwittingly held the keys to the kingdom.

In the Air (2)

(1996)

THE ONLY THING he was nervous about was actually missing his flight. As always, he had left too late and had not counted on the traffic, the parking, the lines, the families checking in with more suitcases than sense, the inefficiency of underpaid employees as well as the unanticipated forces that conspire to make modern travel the mess that it is.

He had traveled enough to know better, but he was young enough to think he would never have to change and not yet old enough to realize he never would. This being more than five years before the day that altered airports forever, he was able to sprint to his gate, and the cabin door was still open five minutes before its scheduled departure. Success.

All on board, another chance to fly the friendly skies, this time to visit a friend on the West Coast. As he settled into his assigned seat this was what he thought about: The next time I set foot on the ground it will be on the opposite side of the country. Dark here, light there, he thought. Cold here, warm there.

...

Not long after the plane was in the air, he noticed a man seated several rows ahead of him. This man, whose face he couldn't see, made him think about his Pops. From where he sat, the man in front of him could very well have been his own father, ten years down the line: the patch of receding hair widened, the gray that had struggled to overtake the brown now wrestling with the white creeping in at all corners.

Someday he's going to be an old man and I'm going to be responsible for him.

Where did that come from? This unprompted realization kicked off an unfamiliar apprehension: the future, assuming his place in the world and all the things over which he exerted only mutable degrees of control.

...

He tried to sleep but was unable to shake the sudden and disconcerting image of his father as an elderly man. As he himself was just entering a period of stability, the prospect of witnessing his father's eventual deterioration was horrifying. Unendurable. It was worse, somehow, than confronting his own mortality. The reason for this, he knew, was that he was cognizant, if not entirely comfortable with his own fragility—the vulnerability of being human—and accepting it. He had never found himself (allowed himself?) to imagine his father revealing a lack of control. He had never known his father to cry, even at the funerals of his own parents. Over time the son had taken for granted that his father was at once inscrutable and incontrovertible: an entity that precluded explanation. In other words, even as he had embraced so many of the assumptions and illusions most adults successfully grapple with at some point, he had scarcely ceased to view his Pops from a child's perspective.

His father, he had figured out many years before, was a piece of work—even for an Irish Catholic of his time and place (post-Depression, Boston). Over time it had become obvious that the only perceptible distress he would betray was the possibility of actually revealing an unguarded emotion, any sign of weakness.

...

"You've *never* seen your father cry?" a girlfriend had asked, a few years before.

"No, I never have," he'd said, deciding to tell the truth.

She hadn't believed him.

"I'm serious," he'd insisted.

"But, how is that possible?"

"Well, he's old school..."

"That's just *weird.*"

"We're not an unweird family."

"The rest of you seem pretty normal."

"You don't know the half of it," he'd said, deciding to tell half the truth.

"So...if your father doesn't cry, what does he do?"

"Uh..."

"I mean, instead of crying, does he show no emotion at all?"

"He's Irish."

"What does that mean?"

"He can do anger, and silence, and he even allows himself to be amused sometimes."

"But what about if...when he's *upset?*"

"He's Irish."

"What does that *mean?*"

"He keeps it locked up in there."

"In there?"

"In the vault."

"The vault?"

"You know, inside."

"That's just weird."

"I don't disagree."

"*You* cry."

"Of course I do; I'm my mother's son."

"So your mom cries?"

"She's Italian."

"You're a disaster! You cry during movies…and not even *sad* movies!"

"You don't know the half of it."

• • •

He did cry during movies. And conversations. He often cried alone, especially when he listened to music. And not even sad music.

(So, you might ask him, are you really suggesting someone should want to listen to music that's capable of making them cry?)

(Yes, he would reply.)

(But, you might ask, why would someone want to do such a thing?)

(It's simple, he would say. So you know you're alive.)

. . .

Now unable to take his eyes from the back of the head of the man who might have been his father, ten years down the line—with his thinning hair and almost imperceptibly sagging shoulders—he realized that he'd come to rely on his father's unflappable manner. Even as he had grown and changed, and gone through some of the transitions that led him—and allowed him—to accept that in many ways he was not like his father, he always could count on his old man's consistency. Perhaps he had, in part, even trained himself, if unconsciously, to condition his temperament and a burgeoning artistic sensibility in contrast to his father's intransigence, which had often befuddled him in earlier years.

He'd never seen his father cry, but who knew what happened when he wasn't watching. He knew his father had been on a plane, alone, visiting his own mother those final times after her stroke: a languid decline, more a resignation than a surrender. And before that, dealing with his own father's death: immediate, unplanned for. At age eighteen and then twenty-one he had watched his father, a man who never forgot to pray and always remembered not to cry, standing over his parents' coffins—first his father's and three years later, his mother's—resolute if not necessarily serene. His father's faith was his safeguard: against emotion, against injustice, against ambiguity; a bulwark against the darkness. He believed in his father's faith; that belief was possibly more strong and secure than the faith his father held.

He had seen his mother cry, and he knew she'd taken several flights of her own—right around his tenth birthday—alone and afraid, anxious yet dreading the idea of seeing her own mother, who was slipping away, too fast and too young.

Left Alone
(1978)

I'M SCARED, I said.

"It's okay," she said. "You know I'll never leave you, right? I would never leave this place without you."

How many times did she tell me that? How many places did she need to remind me that even if I couldn't see her, she was still there? In the grocery store, the shopping mall, a swim meet, even a restaurant. Parents typically didn't use words like agoraphobia back in the late '70s. Maybe they don't use them today, at least around eight-year-olds.

"It's okay," she would say. "You know I would never leave you."

And I did know it. I believed her. It wasn't the fear of being left alone (even an eight-year-old knows it's irrational, even if he can't explain it); it was the fear itself. *It's the fear itself,* I didn't say, because how can an eight-year-old articulate a concept he can't understand? How do you convey the dread, bubbling up like blood from a scraped knee, brought on without warning or reason—the inexplicable consequence of chemistry? Only once it's become established, a pattern, do you remember to expect it, even if you still don't understand it. Anticipation of a word you haven't yet learned and a sensation you can't yet articulate: *anxiety.*

I'll never leave you, she said.

And I believed her. It was never quite enough—in that moment—but it was all she could do, other than never leaving my sight. Even I could understand that. Years and too many close calls to count later, I finally figured out that I had to go through that moment, alone, and then it would never be the same. The fear disappeared and everything would be okay. It was the dread of not knowing, yet being aware it was always inside, that made those moments so difficult to deal with. I had to experience it, get past it, and then this ineradicable fear would subside.

As Opposed to Prayer: A Poem

(2003)

NERVOUS AND UNNERVED this evening, alone:
Searching for solace, something not unlike prayer,
A hope that the past will not repeat itself,
Progress: a preemptive strike, this *procedure*
(They call it a procedure when
They expect nothing unexpected).
Precedence and percentages: our family has a history,
Meaning that some part of someone who has died
Might be alive and unwelcome and somewhere inside.

Remembering: immeasurable moments, IVs and all
The unpleasant things you can't force yourself to forget.
Bad days, worse days, glimpses of serenity then grief,
A flash focus of forced perspective—*this too shall pass.*
Then, inevitably, earlier times: I recall
When doctors and dentists handled us with bare hands.
Still living, then, in a past the future had not
Crept up on, a time when the truth was believable,
Because the only lies that children can tell
Get told to escape tiny troubles they've created.

And so I am uneasy and it's not even myself
I am thinking about: frightened all over again
For my mother, and I can do nothing for her
Now, just as I could do nothing for her, then.
A cycle: she had seen her own mother suffer
While each of them made their anxious inquiries,
Appeals entreating the darkening clouds, out of time.

Like her son, she eventually became acquainted
With the white-walled world of procedures
And all that happens—before, during, after, and beyond:
Hope and fear, faith then despair—the nagging need
To believe in men and the magic of machines.
Or the things we say when no one is speaking.

I'm so scared, she said, to anyone who was listening.
I know I was, and we hoped that God was,
The God who may have done this and a million other things
In His austere, always unaccountable way.
In the end: she feared the truth but not the reasons why
Awful things always happen to almost everyone.
Me, I envied the armor of her fear, I understood
I could not even rely on those lovely lies
About a God I can't bring myself to believe in.

We were there: a child and the man
Who brought me into this calculus.
(We are made in God's image, they say,
But it's your parents' faces you see when
You look at pictures and see the future.)

He said what needed to be said: nothing.
And I said what he said. After all,
What were we supposed to say, the truth?
The truth was this: we too were scared.

I'm so scared, she said, and we told her
It was going to be okay, we told her
We had reason to believe and we told her
Other things when the things we'd already told her
Turned out to be untrue. We never told her
The truth, which was that we were lying.

Fear and faith are useful if you can afford either/
Or, fear is free and lingers always, longer.
After it has served its purposeless point,
Like a stain on the street, days later.
Dying is nothing to be daunted by, it's living
That takes the toll: living with death,
Living with life, being unprepared or unwilling
To be unafraid when it's finally time to die.

I'm so scared, I say, to anyone
Who may be listening in the silence,
Wondering if they can do more for me
Than we could manage to do for her.
There is no one left to lie to—yet
The truth, as always, is immutable.
And so, if you are out there, please help me
To absolve this dread that no one can hear.

A Time for Ghosts (1)
(2002)

SHE SITS ALONE by the window.

The house is soundless as the sun sets, burning the impossible last brightness of its expiring light into the dissolving clouds.

Restless, her eyes never still, she absorbs the silence that holds the house in its unyielding grip. She glances anxiously at the fireplace, its faded red bricks darkened from the heat it has provided; at the old clock shifting its solemn machinery, tracking the time that spun ceaselessly into itself; at the picture hanging on the wall, the faces staring back with smiles frozen in their forever moment. (Seeing herself, younger, full of life. Seeing her mother, younger, still alive.)

She shuts her eyes and feels the truth.

She thinks about her life. She isn't ready to die. It made no more sense now that she was the one unwilling to go, the one everyone else looked at and asked questions about. The one who had to make some kind of reconciliation with an outcome she couldn't control or comprehend.

She hears her son's voice saying, *Is grandma going to die?*

She hears her granddaughter's voice saying, *Are you going to die?*

She hears her own voice saying, *Am I going to die?*

Staring at the Sun

(2000)

I LOOK DOWN at my mother. (*As I lay dying*, I do not think.)

The second surgery. *We're used to this*, I thought. *It won't be as bad as before*, I hoped.

It's worse than I expected. (You don't expect anything; you worry and fear and anticipate and dread and delay and avoid and if you're the type of person who prays you hit your knees early and often, but mostly you prepare yourself as best you can for what you never can prepare yourself to see.) I didn't expect this: I saw my sister, only a few years ago, just after childbirth and while, of course, that was an occasion to celebrate, it was also serious business, she'd undergone a Caesarean just as our mother had with each of us. And, of course, I saw my mother the first time, only a few months after my sister's C-section, in 1997. That was different, as we didn't know it was cancer until after they got inside her. This time is different.

I expected, I suppose, something similar, not thinking (not allowing myself to think?) about the difference between local anesthesia and going *under*, the real differences between a by-the-book medical procedure and a search-and-destroy kind of surgery. She isn't yet able to speak (they wheeled away a frightened

33

woman and brought us back an infant, uncertain how to talk, breathe, or think; that's what those first seconds are like when they let you into the room) and the force of my shock hits me like a sucker punch below the belt. The wind rushes out of me—an innocent bystander anxious to leave the scene of a crime—and the water spills out of my eyes as if someone has flipped a switch. It's not crying so much as a chemical reaction (chemistry? physics? biology? all of the above, including the algebra of anguish), and I'm mortified that my brave, smiling face (*Everything's going to be okay!*) has betrayed me in less than five seconds.

Look at her: spread out under oppressive white sheets like an etherized lab experiment (biology again). Tubes threaded through her nose into her stomach to clean up the mess they make while saving your life. Tubes and wires connected to machines that blink and breathe, electronic chaperones keeping guard over carefully administered fluids. It's all at once impressively state of the art and appallingly primitive. Look how far we've come; we've only come *this* far? And, inevitably: Is this what she saw when she visited her mother, almost exactly twenty years ago? How much worse were the conditions (the prep, the prognosis, the recovery) then? And twenty years before that, her father's father and the colostomy bag he wore for the last decades of his life. Old school: It was unfortunate, but it was miraculous; twenty or so years before that he wouldn't have had a chance. This is progress, this is medicinal intervention being refined before our eyes, stitch by stitch, drip by drip, second by second, each patient another specimen, another insect laid out on the table to be scrutinized, tagged, and, whenever possible, saved.

Where are you?

Did I actually almost faint just now? Are you kidding me with this cliché? (*Get used to it, kid*, I finally find myself saying, not without a little appreciation at the ways situations like these turn unbelievably personal and possibly profound moments into scenes that couldn't even bribe their way into bad movies.) Do I really need to leave the room and splash cold water on my face? Yes, I do.

I rush out into the hallway, past the white coats scurrying here and there, somehow frowning and smiling at the same time, as only doctors can do, and find the bathroom with its sterile, brightly lit sink. Take some deep breaths, just as I've learned to do at times like these. A few moments ago I felt hot; now I'm chilled (the physics of chemistry?). And tired. It wouldn't be a terrible idea to get some fresh air, I think, heading toward the elevator.

On the way down to the lobby it stops and a tall, older man gets in (if I saw him today, ten years later, I'd probably say he was later-middle-aged and maybe, if he had grandkids, they would say I was middle-aged). He looks at me and we exchange a quick, cordial nod. It's a gesture that stops short of being formal, or friendly, but it's considerably different than the look strangers customarily give one another in a public place. The difference, to anyone else, would be all but imperceptible: this exchange of empathy, this implicit solidarity. It's a communication given and received exclusively in hospitals, where no one entering or exiting is free from the peculiar burden compelling their visit.

As I'm walking out I pause and hold the door for a young woman (if I'd seen her ten years ago I would have said she was middle-aged) wheeling an older man (her grandfather? her father? her husband?) hunched over in his chair. She's smiling and she's beautiful. She's beautiful because she's smiling; she has the unforced look of assumed control masking whatever concerns lie beneath. Or maybe she's on her way to figuring out (or has already figured out) the appropriate equilibrium between care and acceptance. Whatever it is, she's beautiful and I hold the door while she slowly slips out from the real world into the sanitized field of dreams and secrets where destinies come to be realized around the clock.

"Thank you," she says, the smile spreading.

Don't go, I want to say, because I've fallen instantly in love.

Strangers can become unwitting saviors to someone who's in crisis. It's not something you (or they) can control; it has to do with the formula that occurs when our biology feels chemistry and does physics. We're scared and in need of assurance; we're vulnerable and desperate for consolation. We're people and need to grasp whatever hands might be reaching out in the dark; we're hoping to be saved by that human touch.

And so I find myself suddenly in love, just as I fell in love with the oncologist in '97 and would fall in love with the nurse from the night shift in 2001—the one I actually sent flowers to (or at least I meant to; I actually wrote down her name with a note reminding myself to send her something to let her know I appreciated her efforts, that some of us realize what a difference people like her make, and that even if all our efforts are ultimately in vain the type of care and concern she provided was never without meaning, and above all that I loved her). The exact opposite of the way I would despise the surgeon in 2002 for laughing (she wasn't laughing at us; she didn't know I could see her, so I had no choice but to forgive her even though I can never forget that moment, in the hallway, seconds before she and her colleague—the one she was laughing with as they walked toward us—delivered that final verdict, the one we had waited for and been able to avert for a little under five years).

...

Outside, at last. I can feel the sun, that unblinking life force. At once imperious and impervious, a warm-blooded bystander to our exigencies, however fervent and fleeting.

I look up, cautiously: You learn not to stare into the sun; it's dangerous and even worse, it's unhelpful. What is the sun going to tell you, even if it cared to acknowledge you, even if it *could*? It's enough that it's there. I'm grateful, at least, for the clarity of its glow, the fact that it does its dirty work during the day, and is kind enough to go away long enough to let the other stars operate under cover of darkness. These stars don't say anything and they don't need to; at least we can *see* them: They're there, no matter where they came from. They were there before we got here and they'll be there long after we're gone. Humbling, maybe even horrifying, but there's nothing we—or they—can do about it. It might not be enough, but it somehow has to be.

> *Tyger! Tyger! burning bright*
> *In the forests of the night,*
> *What immortal hand or eye*
> *Dare frame thy fearful symmetry?*

You learn not to talk to the stars, or you eventually realize it's senseless to hope they can hear you. Yet enough people need to have their actions explained that we made a science of sorts out of animals in the sky, lit with meaning and the ability to govern our affairs the way the moon turns the tides.

Many of us are taught to talk to God, and some of us actually think He's listening. Those one-way conversations are enough for enough people that we sanctify that shot in the dark, that wish upon a star. Enough people need these mysteries explicable that we invest the sky with spirits and wish them into being: They make sense out of what we can't explain for ourselves, and suddenly the senselessness yields salvation.

If all else fails, enough people come to understand and possibly take comfort in the fact that you can always talk to yourself. *You* know who you are, and you'll always hear your voice, even when you don't want to. Even—and especially—when you're not sure what you can tell yourself, when you're not at all certain what you can or should or may say.

In the Air (8)

(1980)

The majority of airline crashes occur in the first twenty seconds after take-off...

As THE PLANE prepared for the flight out of Dulles she repeated the words she'd read, or heard, and then been unable to forget, unsure if they were comforting or some type of cruel compulsion. She didn't like to fly. She hated to fly alone. She could barely get her mind around the idea that she was flying, alone, back to Boston, to be with her mother at the hospital. *I want to be there when she wakes up,* she'd said. *I need to see her when she comes out of surgery,* she'd explained to her husband. *My mother is sick,* she'd told her son and daughter, hoping their father could handle any other questions after she'd left. She thought about her son, whose birthday she was going to miss. He was old enough to understand, which made it easier. She wondered how much easier it would be if he was younger, unable to realize what was happening: no questions, one less thing to try to explain. But then he might never remember her if the plane crashed... No—she couldn't allow herself to go there, not yet.

(What is life, she'd thought as she looked down at her mother, a month earlier, shortly after the diagnosis. *How bad is it?* she'd asked. *It's bad,* her father had said. A flash of preparation, a test of faith. *(My faith is being tested...)* How could this loss be endurable without a conviction that our lives are transitory, part of a process we remain unable to understand? Her mother wasn't ready to die. She wasn't ready for her mother to die. It was too soon, too sudden, nothing to make sense of.)

She held her rosary beads and thought about her son. He'd been disappointed, of course, but he was also excited about his new record player with the built-in speakers. He was young enough to find simple distractions through the things that occupied his time—music, reading, writing, the pictures he used to draw turning into little stories. Mostly, he was still young and she tried to appreciate things for what they were. She had attempted to absorb his vitality and take it with her.

She closed her eyes and thought about her life.

...

Boston. Engaged at twenty-two. She had said yes when he asked her to spend the rest of her life with him, but balked—and almost recanted—when she found out soon after that the moderately well-paying job he'd just landed (right out of college) would require the rest of their lives to begin together in Arizona, over two thousand miles and two time zones away from her family and friends—her life. He may as well have asked her to move to Alaska, or even to Ireland, where she knew his grandparents had emigrated from (hers had come over a few decades later, from Italy). The desert. It couldn't have been more dissimilar from the cracked and well-traveled streets of Boston, a familiar, comfortable landscape—cramped, noisy, even dirty. But that dust and grime was beautiful in its own peculiar way; it was an unmistakable signal of life. A sign of people, and where there were people there was security. Nothing could seem more ominous and oppressive than the vast open spaces and quiet desolation of Flagstaff, Arizona.

Incredibly, it was her own mother who'd done the most to convince her to keep an open mind about this unexpected, undesired rite of passage. *Do you love him?* Very much, she'd replied. More questions. *Do you see this as the man who will protect you and be the father of your children? Why do you think there are jobs for the taking out in places like Arizona?* And answers. Because *that's* where the jobs are; all the jobs here are already taken, and no one is giving them up. Things will be different for you; the days of living in the same town as your parents are passing. Besides, what are you going to do, stay here and marry a milkman?

The last question had been in jest, and they'd both laughed over it, but as years went by, she often thought back on what her mother had said. Not the words so much as what they were meant to signify—*Don't you want to do better than us, to live better than we did?* Meeting and marrying a college graduate was not to be taken lightly—a scientist, even! There are two types of people, her mother said, the people who grow and change, and the people who stay the same. And when you come visit us in a few years, you'll see what I mean, and you'll know what you would have missed if you'd stayed here.

Of course her mother had been right. But once she'd settled into married life, once she was a mother and had established her routine, she would sometimes become distracted—in the middle of an afternoon as she scrubbed the tile walls of their bathroom shower, or while she ironed her husband's work shirts, or while she was cutting up vegetables for that evening's supper—and wonder if she'd made a decision (the most significant decision she would ever make) based on the security and the improved station in life she'd known her husband could supply. And she thought about that milkman, or the postman, or the butcher, or the truck driver, or the cabinetmaker her husband's father had been, and pondered if anyone actually built a life based on passion. The type of love celebrated in the movies. The type of love that made the practical and important things, such as security and careers and propriety irrelevant. The type of love that made sense out of the improbable. The type of love that made life infinitely less complicated, rather than infinitely more so. And in spite of herself, she wanted to believe this love was not attainable, that it was not real. Because it was too overwhelming, even devastating, to think that she was no different after all, that she'd been obliged—by the prevailing and unquestioned culture that surrounded her—to make a decision based on convenience (even as she'd protested that the conditions of their Western relocation couldn't have been more inconvenient). And she resented that possibility. How can one make a decision like that at the age of twenty-two! How is one supposed to be able to make the most important decision of all before she even knows who *she* truly is?

But most of the time she was too preoccupied to consider such alternative possibilities. Being a mother required a mental fortitude that far outweighed and overwhelmed any of the physical duties housekeeping entailed. She wasn't sure her husband, or any husband, was willing or able to grasp this. Certainly they were the ones who woke up every morning and hustled off in their starched collars and freshly shaven chins to conquer the world, or think up new ways to avoid being conquered, or

whatever all these tight-lipped, identically overgrown boys did—
or pretended to do—while they were away from home for nine
hours each Monday through Friday. But when they came home,
despite the fact that they too had an investment in the house, and
the children, they nevertheless were able to define their existence
primarily through their work. And when they came home from
a typical day's toil, in the eyes of those who made the rules we
all live by (who, of course, were also men), they had fulfilled
the expectations their roles required. Everything else—fathering,
lawn-mowing, lovemaking—these were all necessary but *extra*
dimensions. More importantly (and the biggest, most crucial distinction lay in this facility) they didn't have to question *themselves*.
Tossing the football with their boy, raking the leaves in the front
yard, taking their wife out to a nice dinner each Saturday night,
these were nice, even compulsory things, but no man would be
judged too harshly by his proficiency at any of these extracur-
ricular activities. How much his paycheck was, how he coexisted
with his fellow workers, what type of car he drove. *These* were the

inviolable markers of a man's character, particularly in accordance with the mores of the new and rapidly burgeoning middle class.

A woman on the other hand—a *wife*—whose principal duties involved the expedition of domestic accord—cleaning, cooking, and child-rearing—had an altogether different standard by which she was measured. The primary distinction lay in the subtle but unavoidable reality that her duties—her *job*—were not measured or quantified by a time clock that she punched each day. The obligations of motherhood (again, the mental aspects much more than the various, tangible tasks) were predicated upon the understanding (and acceptance) that there was never a moment in which she was absolved, or relieved from her responsibility. Thus, if a woman spent all day cleaning the house and organizing the financial affairs, tending the child and feeding the family, and if, ten minutes before she was ready to fall into bed, the child cried out in its sleep, nothing else that had already been accomplished during the course of that day counted for anything until the current crisis was resolved. And the satisfaction with which the resolution was brought about was the one and only manner by which her job was assessed. In those seconds, or moments, when the next crisis was underway, all else hung in the balance. And to fail to deal with a single incident was to accept the invariable assumption (by her husband, by her friends or herself, by the inexplicable urges that make us always *think*, because we always feel the invisible eyes of others over our shoulders) that she was remiss, that she had failed to hold up her end of the bargain.

And for the man who has envied his wife because she's never been obliged to endure the occasionally disconsolate dread of his redundant routine (how work can make days slip into weeks slip into months slip into years and then suddenly the man is wracked with the abrupt impulse to ensure there's meaning in this cycle), any man who has envied his wife for what he perceives as the opportunity, by virtue of her domestic existence, to avoid or eschew these perplexing inquiries, is exercising misguided judgment. Surely, he has never been on bent knees with a scrub brush, resenting the linoleum floor for demanding to be cleaned only to be sullied again; or cursed the black-soled work shoes (the most expensive pair in the house) that consistently scuff and besmirch, in an instant—a simple trip to the refrigerator for a glass of milk— the sheen that required so much deadening effort to produce. He has never vacuumed a living room floor and wondered how many hundreds of times the same pattern has already been run over this carpet, and how many hundreds of times the same pattern will be run, over the same footprints and crumbs and even the untrodden patches, which nevertheless need to be gone over, for consistency's sake. He has never washed his son's or daughter's hair and caught himself resignedly pondering that at the same time the next day, the wet squeaky hair will be matted and filthy and smell of dust and dirt and mischief. He has never stirred a pot on the stove and caught himself wondering how many other pots, at that very moment, were simmering on other stoves in the neighborhood, in the city, in the country. And perhaps most tellingly, he has never awakened himself in the middle of the night, fighting the urge to rush into his child's bedroom because sometimes the calm silence of a dark room is more frightening with unspoken possibilities than all the tantrums and tears and traumas the daylight's vigilance oversaw.

. . .

She opened her eyes and looked out the window. She'd thought about her past and now she was heading toward it, the plane moving too fast, bringing her to events that were occurring too quickly. She went through a cycle of the rosary, gripping the beads almost unconsciously. This routine, taught to her in childhood, occasionally prompted more vexation than release; this inculcated act of supplication that called to mind previous episodes of pain or fear in her life. She saw herself sobbing before the stern eyes of the priest as she made her first confession—the *Act of Contrition* as it was commonly called. That same priest would admonish the parish to pray for the sick and elderly, and after a while a new concern had crept in—if I pray hard enough can I help them? The morning of her wedding and the unexpected despair she'd felt upon realizing—as she stood before the mirror—that from this day forward she was no longer a girl; that childhood now stood irrevocably behind her. The sight of her husband driving away to work, leaving her alone—and pregnant—in that isolated apartment, moored in the desert. Again, a few years after that, now with another infant (this time a boy), in another new place, just south of the nation's capital. The day, less than a month ago, when her father called to tell her the news none of them could bring themselves to believe. *(How bad is it?* she'd asked. *It's bad,* he'd said.) The day she asked the same question she had feared her son would ask before she left for the airport: *Is she going to die?*

Equivalence

(2002)

ALL THINGS BEING equal, I may be more willing to succumb to the strength or the obverse infirmity that made total belief or nonbelief an option. If there is a God then there could be order, and solace in the notion that there's a plan that I cannot (should not?) comprehend, and that I will be reunited with my mother—with everyone—eventually. Or, if there is no God, then the universe is senseless, random, not particularly malicious (neither justice nor punishment) and the only Truth is the type that man and Nature provide: one could just move on, secure to drift into the darkening distance. But I have neither privilege: the refuge of the faithful or the freedom of the faithless.

What I have are questions. The ones I ask and the ones people ask me:

What happened to your mother?

She died.

What did she die of?

Death.

Any way you describe or explain it, it's ultimately part of a larger equation that now equals nothing.

Life without a mother leaves one with no option but to answer questions with more questions.

Questions:

You know that woman you saw in the grocery store, stocking up on frozen vegetables and paper towels, tissue, and toilet paper for her family? *That was my mother, too.*

That woman who waved at you when you stopped to let her cross the street in front of you? *That was my mother, too.*

That woman who cut you off on the freeway, then flipped the finger when you laid on your horn? *That was my mother, too.*

That woman on TV sewing a blanket for her first grandchild, or bringing out pumpkin pie after Thanksgiving dinner? *That was my mother, too.*

That woman who carried you in her womb, raised you and then sent you off into the world, smiling beneath her tears? *That was my mother…*

Do you see what I'm saying? My mother isn't your mother, but I see a part of her in every mother I see, just as you may see yours all around you someday, if you don't already.

All things being equal, I might never say or even think any of these things. But all things are not equal. All things are never equal.

Q&A

(2013)

QUESTION: WHAT WOULD you do differently?

Answer: Nothing.

True answer: Everything.

Truest answer: I don't know.

...

If the death of a loved one provides the ultimate answer it also prompts all sorts of questions.

The universal ones, for starters: When will I die? How will I die? Why do we die? The personal ones: What will I remember? What might I regret? And ultimately the question that could define the rest of your life: What would I do differently?

What would you do differently?

I've never asked my sister this question. She did everything she could, and in many ways she did more than any of us. She worked the Internet like it was a convention and introduced herself to every article she could find. She obsessively sought all the inside information she could uncover, even if so many short cuts to insight led to locked doors and dead-ends.

(Our mother had been left with the unyielding aftershock of sorrow. When her own mother died everything happened too quickly, without time to facilitate any sort of strategy. She and her six siblings hardly had time to react, much less regret what could have transpired; they never knew what hit them. The cancer that took their mother was like an anonymous assassin: before anyone could look for faces or fingerprints the crime scene was already in the past tense.)

What could we have done differently?

We knew what we were up against, yet still had no idea how little we knew. "If this were ten years ago I would send you on your way," the surgeon said after the first operation, in '97. "But knowing what we know now, I'm recommending a round of chemotherapy. Let's blast your system so the cancer doesn't have a chance to come back."

We wouldn't worry about what we could have done (we thought). We *did* it.

The cancer came back, of course. A second, successful surgery in 2000 didn't give us false hope and couldn't lull us into a false sense of security. This time the surgeon advised radiation followed by chemotherapy, and we knew we were doing all we could do.

Do you think it's going to come back?

That was the question my sister asked me, in July 2001, just before my mother returned for her annual checkup. "No," I told her, truthfully. "She looks good, she feels healthy, we did everything we could do."

This is what I said to my sister, and to myself. They caught it before it spread—again—and then her system got the chemical scrub, again. What possible chance was there that it could find another foothold?

The cancer came back, of course. A third, not entirely successful surgery in 2001 left us no chance to kid ourselves. The prognosis was ugly but not impossible: she was still ready to fight and we would back her up as far down that road as we could go.

Do you think it will ever go away?

That's the question none of us ever asked. We knew it was in there and we knew it wasn't going anywhere. But it could be stalled, it could shrink, it could, hopefully, be managed. There were clinical trials to consider, reasons to think positive thoughts, and always the chance that a miracle might occur.

Here's the thing: what you don't know will hurt you, whether it involves cancer or used cars. Here's another thing: my sister learned more about cancer, symptoms, treatments, and clinical trials in a little over a year than most people could—or could want to—learn in a lifetime. One of my good friends is an oncologist, another has been a hospice nurse. We also lived in an era where the click of a mouse could uncover more detail than a thousand old medical journals. And still, looking back, it's disconcerting how little we knew, how little we still know, how much more we could learn, and how awful it would be if we were ever obliged to do so.

So: we can't change what we couldn't do, or know, or ask, or say. And we collectively recognize, and accept, that all the information in the world may have done next to nothing to change what happened to my mother. We knew enough, and were fortunate enough, to sign her up for some experimental treatments after that third surgery in 2001. The fact that they ultimately proved unsuccessful (too little, too late?) doesn't mean we shouldn't have explored those options; perhaps we could have explored other ones as well.

What could you have done differently?

This is the question we were never able to ask the assorted surgeons, doctors, and administrators. And what would they say, if we had? What *could* they say?

How much more time does she have?

This is the question we asked, as directly as possible, always leaving enough room—for the doctors, for ourselves—to avoid predictions that might be too true or come too soon. The surgeons told us, depending on the way you hear the words (especially in hindsight), as little as they could get away with, or as much as they dared, while steering us as far as possible from an answer we would figure out on our own, eventually.

Machinery (1)

(1997)

WHEN WE'RE YOUNG or healthy enough not to know better, or to need to know any differently, we don't spend a great deal of time pondering the ways our bodies work. We learn in school that our bodies are like machines (or, if religion gets there first, we're instructed that our bodies are borrowed blueprints, at once made in God's image and the perfect alchemy of His divine experiment, begun in the Garden of Eden).

When the body is unencumbered by illness or self-inflicted duress, it works best when it's inconspicuous. We don't necessarily notice when we breathe, swallow, sweat, absorb, or any of the other invisible responses that keep the organs thriving and the synapses firing.

When we're sick, everything changes. So many of these considerations come into focus and we remember what our bodies allow us to take for granted. When we get fevers or infections, we can acknowledge—and appreciate—that the aches and chills, even the coughing and the phlegm, are evidence of our systems in action, combating the viruses and bacteria that might otherwise incapacitate us. We may marvel at the way a body can cure itself:

illness runs its course, scars heal, skin grows, and symptoms dissipate. It's possible that we never feel healthier than when we're recovering from a minor ailment.

A malignant illness, like cancer, obliges a humbled concession to the limitations of any single system's resources. When the body, invaded by an opportunistic cell, starts to turn against itself, we look to medicine—and the professionals paid to dispense it—because we have few other options. Anyone with a sense of history has the perspective necessary to perceive the ways medicine has enhanced our lives.

At one point in our human development we considered bad health or sickness an infestation of evil spirits; later we used remedies such as leeches and burning glass to drain or expel malevolent fluids. And yet, the way we poison our bodies to thwart the cancer inevitably seems more than a little antiquated, even barbaric: chemotherapy can seem like the modern application of a medieval concept. Our method of making the body a less hospitable host and rendering it almost uninhabitable can cause us to question the progress we've made along the continuum of disease and mortality.

If we're not prepared for what cancer can do, this is a blessing of sorts. Being unprepared means we haven't previously had occasion to think deeply about the disease. The initiation makes us look at things differently, and we never again look at the world, our loved ones, or ourselves in quite the same way.

Machinery (2)
(1979)

UNTIL HE PASSED away shortly before I became a teenager, I would see my mother's paternal grandfather, *Nonno*, every few years at his house. His wife died young (a heart attack), so he'd lived the last thirty years of his life alone. In truth, I remember little except impressions and the stories others have told about him. My recollection is that he was fairly short, had pleasantly disheveled white hair, and still spoke with a strong Italian accent. He kept chickens in his backyard and I enjoyed watching them clucking in their wooden house, or as they roamed freely in the grass. Most of all, I recall that his house smelled like piss.

He was diagnosed with colon cancer in his early sixties and, almost miraculously for that time, the surgery was successful. As a result, he was obliged to wear a colostomy bag and his diet, for the last two decades, existed almost entirely of cereal and crackers. Looking back I can better appreciate what a tough, self-sufficient man he was. He was in poor enough health that he could occasionally have trouble making it to the bathroom. As a result, he simply filled up half-gallon milk cartons and would leave them around the house, mostly in his bedroom.

I was too young to process this on any sort of rational level, but old enough to find it unsettling, and even a little frightening. What I couldn't possibly appreciate, then, was how independent and resourceful he managed to be. I like to think of him living out his years, comparatively content to exist on his own terms, at least as much as he was capable of doing.

All I knew, circa 1979, was that I was going to live forever. I was nine years old, knew nothing of cancer, or old age, infirmity, or isolation. I knew that piss smelled unpleasant, especially when it sat in a semi-open container, neglected inside a warm room within a house without air conditioning toward the end of summer.

I didn't know much in 1979, but most of all I didn't know all that I didn't know, which is the one irretrievable condition of youth. I knew some things, like the fact that my backyard was Fenway and Yaz never struck out; I knew about block parties, blue gills, burned marshmallows, mosquitoes, and putrid bug repellant that didn't kill anything but made me stronger. I knew I was going to live forever and no one close to me was close to dying either. And then, in 1980, Nonno's daughter-in-law, my grandmother, was diagnosed with cancer.

In the Air (4)

(1980)

IT HAD GOTTEN worse in a hurry. Or, already awful and discovered too late, it was busy proceeding at its own pace. Their worst fears had been confirmed; the cancer had spread and was moving too quickly to contain. There's a reason, she realized, that moments like this are so unconvincing or wretched in movies—because they were the same way in real life. How do you handle that news? How do you brace yourself for something you can't imagine? What do you say when you hear the words *weeks not months?* How do you explain it to your children? How do you explain it to yourself?

This time her family was with her on the plane. It wasn't as comforting as she'd thought it would be. Alone with her own dread and uncertainty, she could at least focus on herself, saying and thinking as little as possible, conserve her energy, stay as positive as she was capable of being. Looking at her daughter and her son, she struggled—again—with whether it had been wise to bring them along. *I'm not sure the kids should see your mother like this,* her husband had said. *I want them to see her before it's too late,* she'd replied. *I need them to remember her, even if this isn't the way any of us would prefer it.* And I want her to see *them*, she thought. It can only do her good to be surrounded by people not wearing scrubs and uniforms asking her questions, or being unable to answer the questions she asked. She needs her family right now; she should see what she helped create. *I* need my family right now, she knew. I can't face this by myself.

She closed her eyes and thought about her life.

. . .

They were only out in Arizona for two years, but in that relatively short time (which, more often than not, seemed interminable) she had her first experiences as a wife, mother, and stranger. The first two she was somewhat prepared for, but she couldn't have imagined or prepared herself for how drastic the culture shock would actually be.

She had grown up in a large, close family, and having been the oldest daughter, she wasn't unfamiliar with the tedium of tending to infants. In fact, there was little she hadn't encountered or heard about at one point or another. And yet, in her mind—even in the days before she met her husband, when she used to contemplate her eventual role as a mother—she never once imagined raising a child away from her own parents and family.

In the course of less than a year, she'd gone from living at home, in the city, to getting engaged, married, and moving to the arid expanse of a Western state. Within a month of living in Flagstaff—before either of them had fully adjusted to the climate, time zone, or temperament of their new environment—she discovered she was pregnant. Their excitement was mutual and not inconsiderable; now, at least, she would have something upon which to focus and dedicate herself during the peculiar solitude the days presented her with.

She quickly discovered, however, that being alone and pregnant only exacerbated an overwhelming feeling of isolation and helplessness. Nothing, not even the life she could feel growing inside of her, could compensate for the fact that it felt as though she had moved to a foreign country. Being two thousand miles from home was so abrupt and incomprehensible that it was almost tolerable, the novelty and newness of it.

Each week she could assemble a mental list of the differences between this quiet city near the desert and the frenetic city where she'd grown up. The foods and spices she was used to preparing meals with were not to be found in the grocery store; the one movie theater showed a steady and exclusive stream of old westerns; every restaurant seemed to serve Mexican food (by the time she and her husband left Arizona she had completely lost her taste for any type of southwestern cuisine); the people of the town, although friendly enough, clearly were used to—and comfortable with—the slower, more predictable pace of the fledgling suburban sprawl.

She found that the altitude, combined with her pregnancy, made spending time outdoors exceedingly difficult, so she mostly stayed inside her modestly sized and furnished apartment. And since the scenery—a panorama of the mountains sprawling and stretching from left to right on the horizon—was so awesome, being resigned to view it from her living room became increasingly dispiriting. Even the sunshine began to feel boring, then indifferent, and, finally, overbearing. It never rained, and the sun's rays, the lines that slipped through the windows and dissected her carpet, began to resemble prison bars. After a while, the mountains also began to seem onerous and confining. From the perspective of a cramped and stifling kitchen, or balcony, taking in the silent severity of an uncommunicative landscape was more desolate than being ensconced in a city high-rise. Having grown up around the discordant din of an urban honeycomb, hearing noise and the unintelligible interaction of people's voices had a comforting effect. Silence, she found, was fatiguing. It was the lack of stimulation, the lack of *conflict* that made her feel trapped inside her own thoughts.

Having no one to talk to forced her to focus her energies on two diversions she'd to this point had only a minimal acquaintance with—writing letters and reading books. She wrote letters to her mother, to her sisters, and eventually to herself. Her journal helped distract her from the all but intolerable silence that filled the days in which she was alone, with her thoughts and without her husband. The public library down the road became her salvation; she filled her hours with all the books she'd never gotten around to reading, and all the wonderful new discoveries, all those kindred spirits who commiserated with her. They understood her, and she them. It was through this intriguing method of communication that she understood, and became convinced, that it wasn't words, but those writers' souls on the pages of those well-worn paperback novels. She could finally fathom, in a way that the church services had never sufficiently revealed, the ways in which God imbued His people with an unquenchable ardor, a solidarity that transcended words and actions—a celebration of one's soul.

...

All those souls. She opened her eyes and looked out the window, then at her children. She thought back to her childhood, the church, seeing the stained-glass windows. Those saints in their exultant splendor surrounding the church on every side, a multi-colored fortress. *Time will not forget you*, those eyes said. Silent, serene in their refractive shrines. And when the priest spoke the solemn incantation, in words foreign to her impressionable ears, she imagined that the souls somehow descended into those synthetic designs, gracing the assembly with their divine presence. It was possible to conceive anything in those mystical moments. Words awakening feelings, *that* feeling—the certainty of God's existence, proof in the soul. The conviction that there was only one way to live; the rest would be accounted for.

Written and Unread

(2010)

A VISION:

I'm reading words written by a dead person. Nothing unusual about this; it's practically the story of my life. In this case, however, the person who was still living when these words were written is my mother. Words not intended for my eyes, I know.

Or are they?

All these words, something to which my mother could devote her attention; all that available time that required killing to make it pass more quickly—to make it pass, period. All those hours to fill, especially in the days when we didn't have five hundred channels to choose from or electronic access to a wide, webbed world. All that boredom, all that solitude, alone with her thoughts, alone with herself. All the unappealing emotions we're better equipped to avoid when we have peace, or at least perspective. All the feelings that ultimately find their way out the only way they can: awkwardly, unabashedly, irrevocably. All those sad songs of uncultivated passions, unexplored options, hours and hours of isolation that turn into tiny eternities. All those entreaties to an indifferent world: both confession and accusation, settling old scores and soliciting understanding—or at least empathy—from people who could not be reached, or were no longer around, or who never existed in the first place. All the other people who were busy living while she was busy trying not to die. The dread of nothingness and, eventually, the suspicion that a thing that could be so awful was still ending too suddenly.

Who will remember us?

This is the question implicit in all these words, addressed to God, or Nobody, or Anybody who might be willing to listen. This is the question that can't be answered except by words and deeds and memories that will occur after we're gone. This is the origin of our primordial impulse to connect and believe we stay associated, somehow, some way, after we're no longer able to interact on human terms. This, perhaps, is what ran through her mind once her eyes closed and she stayed asleep, already in another place, still hoping to apprehend some of the miracles she had or hadn't happened to miss during her life. This is the final question that, scrubbed of its universal and spiritual covering, asks explicitly and directly: *Who will remember me?*

. . .

In the fifth grade, encouraged by a teacher, I began to keep a journal. This practice, initially an assignment, became a compulsion that continued on and off for the next two decades. I seldom feel an urge to revisit these hand-scribbled artifacts, equal parts lack of interest and the likelihood of embarrassment that such necessarily solipsistic exercises would induce. But more importantly, I don't need to read the words since I remember writing them and can readily recall the circumstances that inspired them.

Journals, as I see them—and utilized them—come to function as adult versions of diaries, where the purpose is less a regurgitation of events and more a one-way conversation with oneself and, by extension, the world. For me, journal writing served as a self-fulfilling sort of therapy before I even knew what that word meant. The act of trying to make sense of life and, by extension, myself, in writing that was never intended for other eyes.

I wasn't aware, until after she'd died, that my mother kept journals of her own. Knowing her as intimately as I did, I'm neither surprised nor unable to imagine what themes and concerns inexorably resurface throughout her personal narrative. The catalyst to write, whether it's rooted in an effort to justify or interrogate, is primarily an attempt to get whatever it is *on record.* Certainly the longing to relate, on a human level, permits us to unburden ourselves, whether this interaction involves friends, spouses, or counselors. I know my mother frequently utilized all these outlets and some of the time it helped. (I'd like to think it was most of the time but I can't know and I won't kid myself.) Regardless, she was still compelled to document her hopes, fears, and disappointments on paper, and that fact is its own commentary on how reliable she found her various support systems.

I'm not especially inclined to read these words. They weren't addressed to me, and I'm aware that they were intended as an outlet that couldn't adequately quell her discomfort, then, and no longer exists for her, now. My sister found some of these journals and couldn't resist the temptation to read them. She wasn't looking for them; her discovery occurred as part of the aftermath, during the process of going through items my mother left behind. My sister, at that time, wanted a piece of everything our mother had touched, anything she could put her hands on. Predictably, she was unnerved by the experience of reading our mother's words, an experience that's destined to disappoint because all possibility of responding is eliminated.

I asked my sister the same question I ask myself: Why would you want to read about her fights with us, or our father, her friends, or herself, or the ways she could never quite ameliorate the misgivings she had regarding all those usual suspects: her weight, her career—or lack thereof—the people who disappointed her or the fulfillment that eluded her, or her ongoing, ultimately unsuccessful attempt to reconcile the early loss of her mother, et cetera?

I don't need to read about those things in part because I saw so much of them as they unfolded in real time. I remain grateful that I was able, as I slouched toward maturity, to be an open ear and ally. Instead of requiring support the way only a child does, I had the opportunity to reciprocate; to encourage her and listen as often and best as I could. Once I was earning my own paychecks I could finally buy her dinner and listen to her questions and concerns. I reassured her the hard work had already been done, that her efforts and dedication were beyond reproach. All you need to do now, I'd say, is focus on the rest of your life: be a grandmother, develop some new hobbies, and enjoy the peace you've struggled to earn. This was, as is the case with most of us—particularly homemakers whose children have left home—a work in progress. Progress was being made, and then cancer came calling.

An Impossibly Clean Place
(1997)

SHE OPENED HER eyes and took in her surroundings. The tan and turquoise wallpaper, an innocuous, neutral design of flowers and trees. The curtains covering the window were yellow and annoyingly, almost unbearably bright. It was as though in the effort to project a tranquil atmosphere, they could disguise the fact that people were brought here against their will, or obliged by an infirmity that compelled medical attention or treatment that could not otherwise be administered.

But you couldn't fault them for trying.

How different it was compared to the old days! All white. So white it was disturbing—white sheets, white walls, white curtains, white tiled floor. Doctors and nurses, of course, dressed in white. Their white teeth grinning as you looked into the whites of their eyes as they assured you everything was fine. White, white, white. It was, of course, supposed to convey the security of cleanliness—an environment where ill health, germs, bad karma, anything *unsavory* would be overwhelmed and subdued. Nevertheless, it was no place to get *well*; that was for certain.

And yet, considering all this cultivated congeniality, she understood that the stripped-down, utter lack of pretension of the old hospital rooms possessed its own efficacy, the stark comfort of honesty. No promises were made, but the people were there to do a job. Dirty work in an impossibly clean place. It was so honorable, so meddlesome. So human. The business of battling death was not inherently beautiful, nor did it strive toward that aim. It was objective, without a tolerance—or need—for opinion or reaction.

. . .

She hears a voice and looks up to see a woman standing over her, frowning. She hears the woman clearly—a nurse—but the woman's tone indicates that she doesn't think her patient is able to understand what she said.

She opens her mouth and discovers she can't speak. She panics, thrashing around on the bed, attempting to lift herself. She gasps for air and tries to look up at the nurse, who seems to have disappeared.

Everything disappears, and then she herself is no longer there.

Family History (1)
(1940s)

BOSTON. IN THE WINTERS the cold stalked you, stealing your warmth by using the wind. Especially at night in a not-warm-enough house—that dark chill arrived and never left. Winter days that were a dull, gray cloud hanging over the city, clinging to bodies and buildings like a leech.

The bond with her mother had been intense and, for almost two years, uninterrupted. Her father left for the war before she was born and didn't return until she was old enough to under-stand what she'd been missing. Reunited, two parents and one child; she experienced love but also fear. Her first memories of her father were a blur of smiles and silence. A child, through no fault of her own, sees—and senses—when something isn't quite right. The development of an awareness that becomes instinctual, certain words, certain looks that indicate when a father should be left alone, or avoided altogether. Indifference followed by ever-shifting signals of affection. The child not only becomes cogni-zant of, but sensitive to the tense sounds of a quiet house. The more still and silent a house, the more frightening everything that this silence signifies becomes. Certain things that a child learns to fear become things that can never be forgotten.

. . .

Later, she understood her father had his own fears. The fear of God, the fear he might lose his job, the fear that he could be replaced. The fear of getting hurt or losing his house. The fear of some circumstance that would prevent him from being a husband, father, and *man*. He was a difficult man, a *hard* man. This was not a choice he made but was, rather, the result of experience and expectation: the worse those factors had been—for him, for fellow sons of immigrants—the harder he became. An austere, inextinguishable specter of poverty hung around every happy thought, an inescapable component of their existence. His doubts: would there always be work? Without a job there was no money, and without money there was no security. No security meant death. Providing security was a source of identity. *The* source. For a man, no worse affliction loomed than being unable to provide for his family. No excuses, laments, or regrets could be offered to counteract this truth. It is this solitary burden that equates to silence, and fear. And, occasionally, anger.

The chronic angers of that house. Much later, she came across a poem that helped explain him, and made more sense of her unwelcome memories. It usually requires the scope of perspective and distance—from one's parents; from one's childhood—to recognize the redemptory grace that a man who always put his family first is entitled to receive.

> *Sundays too my father got up early*
> *And put his clothes on in the blueblack cold,*
> *Then with cracked hands that ached*
> *From labor in the weekday weather made*
> *Banked fires blaze. No one ever thanked him.*

...

Nonno. He wasn't a complicated man: he had struck a balance, and proudly considered himself an American, but he wasn't far enough removed from the old traditions to expect more than he was entitled to, and she'd never known him to question the life he'd made for himself. His accent was so strong it seemed he was speaking a different language. His hands were workman's hands, with the maps of labor and care imprinted on their clear, creased palms. Hands that had touched the earth, produced and created. Hands, she imagined, like God's hands—large, ancient, capable of molding and shaping the world to their design. His eyes were dark, like his close-cropped hair.

His son, her father, loved to work, and he was proud of the post office. He thought he had the greatest job in the world, even in the early days when he delivered mail in the city, on foot, wearing his scuffed and ragged boots through the slush, coming home to soak his callused feet in the bathtub. He never

complained; he would say that every day in the city he saw people who reminded him how bad things could be, and how fortunate they were.

. . .

Childhood. The nights she would wake up, frightened and alone.
In the middle of the night you heard all the things you didn't
notice during the day. The refrigerator's internal engine talking
to itself; the floorboards shifting and stretching; the wind and
all the creatures outside that came to life when the sun went
away; the house, straining against the burden of holding itself
together. And then the other noises, the old ghosts, the spirits
talking, knowing you won't sleep, or making sure you can't sleep
so you'll hear them. How she would get out of bed and lean her
head against the window, feeling its cold surface on her brow.
Looking into the night sky and sensing her superstitions, carried
over from her earliest memories. Those voices—was there ever a
time when they weren't part of her? Had she simply discovered
a way of remembering those who had gone before, preserving
those lives in her memory? She knew they were connected to her
in ways that death and time could not touch. She was connected
to these feelings the way the sublime images in the stained glass
were connected to the saints we sing about. The way the sun's
rays, captured in that glass, refracted light and warmth through
the church—God's light, giving life to that glass, just as He gave
life to our souls. If you prayed carefully enough He would hear
you. If she listened attentively enough the house itself could
speak to her. The voice, languid, aware, seemed to whisper as
though it understood the lives inside it would eventually expire,
like candles that have burned through the night.

Biology

(1997)

I PULL A chair over to the side of the bed and sit silently, holding my mother's hand. I want to be there when she wakes up. *But what if she doesn't wake up?* No. I don't need to think about that, not now. Not yet.

I close my eyes and hear voices. Old voices, from the past. The old ghosts. As long as I've heard these voices I've respected my obligation to listen, preserving their stories in my memory. My mind: where do the voices come from? Are the old ghosts really speaking through me, or are they propelled by my fancy, products of my imagination? No. These voices have always spoken to me, and I have never doubted them. I have felt, always, part of a life that's bigger than me. And while it's difficult to explain it, these ghosts—lives that expired before I knew them—have always been within me. In my mind, in my memory. Certainly I'm different, but that difference—believing in these voices—has always been my strength, my faith.

My faith is being tested...

Later, I stand outside, thinking about my life.

Above me the stars, in their serene discourse with the darkness, seem to hold the secrets I struggled to understand. Glimmering, so far away, that light: sending messages in a coded, unfathomable language.

...

What did I know about death? If you counted books and movies, plenty. If you limited it to actual experience, very little. I was too young and uninvolved during my mother's mother's death, in 1980, to perceive much beyond the simple fact that her dying made me very sad. I also understood that my grandmother was entirely too young to die and even if, at ten, I hadn't necessarily grasped this, I now had my mother's brush with death, at age fifty-five, to remind me.

The most recent funeral, my father's mother, whom I called Grammy, had occurred just six years earlier, in 1991. This one had been more difficult for me, for more than one reason. Obviously, as a twenty-one-year-old I knew exactly what was happening. More, I understood what was happening before it happened and, worse, understood what would happen after it happened. This is precisely the sort of insight a ten-year-old is incapable of processing, which is ultimately best for all involved. It was a difficult funeral for my father for all the readily discernible reasons, but I knew it was hitting my father hard because I knew how to read my old man. My father was showing less emotion than usual, which at best (or worst) was less than little.

(It was what it was, and I had slowly started to reconcile this reality as an unalterable component of our relationship. My father was a product of his era, just as his mother had been very much a product of hers, only more so. This was a woman who had come from a family that measured how little they had by calculating how much less they would have if they'd stayed in Ireland, which made them more or less identical to every family that had emigrated in the latter years of the last century. This was a woman who, as a young girl, had stood with her classmates after school and pretended she didn't recognize her uncle as he lurched, inebriated, down the sidewalk in the middle of the afternoon. The same uncle who'd been knocked unconscious by his brother—who happened to be a priest—for stealing the family turkey on Thanksgiving. The same uncle who played his ignoble part as the proverbial town drunk although, in fairness, every town had more than one drunk per town in those days, which made it more or less identical to every other town in America then, or now. The secret to my father, I knew, could be best understood by having a better understanding of this woman. The things that shaped him and the feelings that got caught in his throat could mostly be traced back to this woman, the same woman who had grown up to be a grandmother, thereby expunging the past and deflecting all outward signs of discontent into a post-maternal amity, which made her more or less identical to every woman who eventually found herself being called a different name once her children had children.)

Unlike my father's father's death three years earlier, which had been both sudden and unexpected, Grammy's death had been prolonged by several months of extreme, occasionally stark discomfort. It was as though a lifetime's reserve of fortitude and old-fashioned force of will had cracked like a frozen pond in spring, finally freeing her from a self-imposed stoicism. It wasn't quite accurate to describe her death as a *relief*, but it wasn't unfair to say it was, in many regards, welcomed—not least by my grandmother. It had long since become clear that, for understandable reasons, she'd never recovered from the shock of losing her husband. During this last year her physical and spiritual states had deteriorated rapidly. Too rapidly. This couldn't be inexplicable to anyone, considering how abruptly she'd lost the man she'd spent half a century with.

Her funeral had been difficult; more so than my grandfather's, which seemed incongruous since we'd had time to prepare for hers. I could appreciate what my father was dealing with: in the last four years he'd watched his son leave for college and then lost his parents, one after the other. So I'd braced myself for the possibility (inevitability?) that this was the occasion I would finally witness my father crying, even if it was no longer something I desired to see. Not now, not under these circumstances.

I was, nonetheless, unsurprised when my father displayed the same intransigence he'd exhibited at the first funeral. It might have been a relief, in its way, but rather than easing my mind that this was simply the way my father operated, it became excruciating to observe. Because I knew my old man was struggling, and I could hardly comprehend the type of effort this mindset necessitated. It was as though I could actually see my father hardening before me, clinching every muscle to restrain the grief imploding inside him.

(Where does it go when you won't let it escape? Does it work its way out at night, in dreams? Can you kill it with beer, or enough TV, or the ultimate antidote, religion? Can you pray that pain away, and ask God to cast a benevolent spell, transporting those concerns you can't afford to release? Do you just cover your eyes and close your mouth, forcing those feelings to suffocate slowly, with no chance to abscond?)

There was a reception afterward, at the same establishment we'd gone to three years earlier, which lent a solemn symmetry to the occasion. When it was time to offer a toast to the departed, my old man stood up. "She is the last vestige from a very different time, a disappearing time," he pronounced. "We won't see her kind again anytime soon, if ever." He went on to say some other things, but being a man of few words, the speech was short and dutiful, if respectful. I couldn't help noticing the words *love, son,* and *God* were never spoken.

Transformation
(1980)

WE VISITED MY grandmother the spring she died. I didn't know she was going to die, but everyone else did, especially her. I knew she was sick. I knew before I got there that she was *very* sick and I understood the urgency of my mother's recent visits. I realized that this family trip would usually have occurred at the end of summer, instead of while I was still in school.

I remember that she was unable to join the extended family—there were at least a dozen of us in the dining room—and the meal was, obviously, awkward. More, during every previous visit *she* had been the one cooking, talking, coordinating. She was, to me, not only the ideal grandmother (gregarious, ebullient, generous), she was an ideal human being. That, I realize now, is a grandmother's *purpose*—to be a real-life fairy-tale heroine for the children in her world. Toys, treats, and extreme indulgence were seldom in short supply every single time I was in her presence. But it wasn't just her ability to pamper; *everyone* adored her: my grandfather was, after almost four decades, still crazy about her. In fact, to this day I've never seen a husband who looked at his wife the way he looked at my grandmother, like a besotted schoolboy.

She had eased into the role of grandmother in part because she'd already mastered the role of wife and mother. Whether this observation betrays the subjective or naïve reminiscence of a spoiled grandson, the fact remains that no one in that family—especially my mother, as I subsequently and frequently saw first-hand—ever came close to recovering from her death.

The kids eventually went out to the living room to give her kisses. She was pleasant but past the point of putting on a brave face. She was suffering, and while I couldn't fathom what was really going on, I knew I'd never seen anyone appear the way she did, noticeably thinner, weaker and—for the first time in my memory—silent.

Looking back as an adult, I understand that she *was* doing what she could, for our sakes. She would have been in her bed, not on the couch, if we hadn't been visiting, covered in the same heavy blanket on a warm evening in early June. She wouldn't have done something I'd never seen her do, something that was beyond my limited comprehension: force a smile. It was devastating her to separate herself from the socializing she typically oversaw, but she was aware, however resignedly, that it was a result of the cancer that was killing her.

I hugged her, uncomfortable with this new and not-improved version of the woman I loved so unreservedly. Selfishly, I didn't like this change and the things it was already doing to everyone around her. "I hope you feel better," I said. *Maybe she'll look better the next time I see her,* I thought.

Less than a month later we were in Boston, again, for her funeral.

Discursion: Deconstruction

IL N'Y A pas de hors-texte.

Or, there is nothing outside the text.

If the names Barthes, Foucault, and Saussure (for starters) mean nothing to you, it would be difficult to argue that you're missing much. And yet: in the autumn of 1992, I spent more time with these gentlemen than I did with actual, living people. You see, they were all literary theorists, and they were all dead. I arrived at grad school expecting to become more intimately acquainted with some of my favorite Russian authors and dive deeper into American literature.

This happened to be right around the time that Cultural Studies had infiltrated English departments with the fervor of a rotavirus. It's tempting to say I was unlucky in this regard; as it happened, I was also fortunate, in ways I did—and didn't—perceive at the time. To put it as plainly as possible, if the circumstances had been different, the likelihood that I would be writing these words right now is less than remote. I almost certainly would be, if I was lucky enough, a tenured professor. I also, most likely, would be well into my second decade crafting articles for scholarly journals that not even my friends would read, nor would I, being a good friend, want them to.

Long story short: after initially resisting the jargon, the unending analysis (which was initially like watching a Fellini movie on mushrooms), and the impenetrable pretension, I was, for a time, converted. Once the signifying pieces fell into place, I began to appreciate the maddening method of making molehills into mountains. Post-structuralism can quickly become a metaphysical cult, and once the scales fall from your eyes, you embrace the oddly cathartic notion that there will be a ceaseless stream of scales to be pulled off every day for the rest of your life.

As a result, like a soldier who has spent time on the front line, these experiences informed my subsequent relation to reality. Today, I carry deconstruction like a tool in my trunk anytime I need to change a flat tire in my critical acumen. For a while there, I wasn't sure I'd be able to read, much less write fiction ever again. Eventually, I learned how to think without seeing myself thinking, but it took many years to sluice all that onanism out of my system.

What are they after?

I came away from this experience mostly unsullied, intellectually speaking, and am glad for it (the experience and the lack of permanent damage). I came away convinced that, when it comes to art, theory and philosophical concerns certainly have an important place, but not at the expense of the work itself. Perhaps this is why, to this day, I find that actual writers compose the most insightful and convincing reviews and appraisals of fiction (and nonfiction, for the most part). Maybe, if I were to deconstruct my own line of thinking, I'm unintentionally (or purposefully) prejudicing my perspective as the more thoughtful, balanced one. Regardless, academia is, in its extremes, like any cult: it is usually worthwhile to avoid any group convinced they have figured out the secrets of the universe, particularly when the answers involve the creation of more, unnecessary questions.

ii.

Toujours déjà.

What are we after?

From the moment my mother stopped living, everything that has happened can, of course, be measured along the continuum of before and after. But being alive, still, I now am unable to recall anything that happened before without some awareness that she is dead—that she will die. This happens in the abstract (the knowledge is there, which doesn't change the memory, but it alters, however subtly, the process of remembering), but it also affects specific times and dates: I will recall an event from 1998 and some part of me thinks—or is simply aware in advance—how she will be gone in four years. An occasion from early 2002 will prompt the troubling question: eight months left; she had no idea and neither did we. And so on.

It gets even more complicated during dreams. And that's only addressing the ones I remember, and the ones I remember remind me that most of us are dreaming constantly, endlessly, every night, creating screenplays and scenarios, concocting future stories while revisiting past mistakes or triumphs or slipping darkly through the glass into impossible escapades—the type that could only happen in heaven, or dreams, or a Fellini movie.

In these dreams and in my memories my mother is *always-already* deceased. Toujours déjà. I am *always-already* predisposed to deal with her death, just like I can't remember attending church without the eventual loss of faith, or my post-graduate studies without the abrupt decision to flee the ivory tower, or my on-going quest to construct mysteries I might solve only through writing.

Mostly, perceiving existence through this lens applies to looking forward as well as looking backward. Knowing, ahead of time, how certain decisions or actions are likely to play out (based on experience, based on characters from books, based on intuition) obliges one to avoid clichés. This insight, a sort of prognostic radar, can be as paralyzing as it is liberating: you don't want to make any moves that will contribute to a life someone else already lived, but you also don't want to preclude the fortuity of chance. If you think too much you can outsmart the future, or else become Bartleby, preferring to do nothing in order to preserve the illusion of an unfettered free will.

iii.

The living owe it to those who no longer can speak to tell their story for them.

Czeslaw Milosz, one of the great artists of the last century, was a poet as well as a professor. He could appreciate literature from both angles: the creation of it as a writer and the inspection of it as a reader. Having seen some of the atrocity humankind was capable of during his lifetime, his work uses words to elegize, accuse, and above all to remember. His great obsession was doing his part to ensure that the suffering and the bravery and the cruelty were a little less possible to ignore and forget. His poetry, in part because of its brilliance but mostly because of its restraint, all but resists analysis: he knows what he's trying to say and you know what he's trying to say. It's more than that; it's always more than that. Like all the best poetry, the deceptively simple words are fraught with feeling and affect. You cannot, in short, deconstruct Czeslaw Milosz.

I came across a poem of his that I strongly suspect would have affected me in a profound fashion whether I encountered it before or after grad school. It does, nevertheless, seem to epitomize—with astonishing clarity and conciseness—what miserable if well-meaning theorists spend chapters and careers agonizing to articulate half as well.

> *What I know of my laborious life: it was lived...*
> *I don't need to write memos and letters every morning.*
> *Others will take over, always with the same hope,*
> *The one we know is senseless and devote our lives to...*
> *So the Earth endures, in every petty matter*
> *And in the lives of men, irreversible.*
> *And it seems a relief. To win? To lose?*
> *What for, if the world will forget us anyway.*

Poets and professors are ultimately in search of similar things: not necessarily the answers to specific questions but the process of discovering, and interrogating the things that perplex us. It's not the answers or even the questions but the act of investigating: that dissatisfaction; not an act of rebellion or defiance, but an appreciation and, ultimately, acceptance that we can't know. We can never know but we must try.

This, it seems to a former altar boy and once-future scholar, is the most satisfactory elucidation of what impels us to learn and love and live.

Beethoven (1)

(1987)

AWAKE, ALIVE. ALONE.

Never forget this feeling.

That evening, halfway through high school, watching the snow fall outside your window. Lights out and *that* music playing: Beethoven. The sonatas, with titles that seemed mysterious and exhilarating: *Pathétique, Appassionata, Mondschein.*

The music, it seemed, was always there for these significant moments: remembering those times, always accompanied by music that was solemn yet ecstatic. Later on, being ushered into the other worlds of sexual activity, or studying for fast-forgotten exams, or those solitary seconds that sometimes turned into hours, the time alone, in the darkness, before sleep overtook awareness and you still knew who you were—tracing it all back to that first evening, staring at the snow: the sound of the piano, feeling connected to lives apart from your own, able to imagine what the world was like, *then*, feeling deeply aware of your own life, wholly there, utterly cognizant—which, of course, did not mean you were only aware of yourself; it was exactly the opposite sensation—and not realizing, not needing to know, yet, that this feeling would be increasingly difficult to capture, transitory moments of perception as a tonic for, or distraction from, the muddle of adult life and the urgency and oddness that this new reality entailed. It was not that this music facilitated these feelings, but that it accompanied them. This was what made it central to your world, so inextricable from your soul, from the way you wanted to see yourself.

Christmas

(1990)

IT'S NOT A DREAM. It really is going to be a White Christmas, in Virginia.

A miracle, he thinks, sardonically, and then frowns. This was a mistake, he realizes as the snow flings itself at his windshield and the road disappears in a white swirl.

You can't go home again, he thinks, and then smiles in spite of himself. He hasn't been back to his church, or any church, for a while.

Too long for your own good. He can hear his father's tacit displeasure as the car idles diffidently, ready to go wherever he'll take it. The stained glass depiction of the Last Supper, which at one time had inspired such conciliatory thoughts, now seems vaguely portentous as it looms above him in the darkness, like a billboard. The day has come and gone, he understands, when the simple act of attending mass would bestow upon him the ecumenical grace reserved for the very young and the elderly.

He hesitates, still unsure if he wants to enter the church, which will soon be overcrowded with stout believers and casual once-a-year attendees, all seeking to mollify their joys, fears, and guilt, the combination of which forged the enigmatic foundation of their enigmatic faith. Eventually, he opens the door and pauses in the cold corner at the back of the church. Despite his misgivings, he finds he's unprepared for the force of his ambivalence. It's neither relief nor disappointment, simply the lack of resolve. He starts to sit down, but feels oddly unwelcome as he surveys the empty rows of seats, at last understanding the essence of his isolation: as much as he's tried, he is not like his father.

Throughout his childhood he attended mass regularly, and like chores or homework, it eventually became an expected part of his routine. He even served as an altar boy, like his father had done before him—back in the day when it was a *real* mass, performed in Latin, a fact of which he was often reminded. Even as he grew older, and the novelty began to wear off, the weekly ritual was not without its attendant grace, and he still anticipated the cathartic gratification dispensed upon those who chose to receive the gift of the Eucharist. The passion and pain, creation and salvation in less than an hour, consistently alleviating an unusual burden, as though an otherwise unattainable clemency had been granted.

Closing his eyes, he makes a feeble attempt to pray, but finds he's unable to shake the sudden, disconcerting vision of himself standing on the altar while the congregation kneels before him in their finest clothes, reading the solemn Word of God, written with the intent of keeping them subdued and submissive. Instead of leading the assembly in a reading of the scriptures, he envisions himself speaking out, interrupting them, a Saint Paul in reverse, declaring his anti-conversion. Would the stunned assembly, faces he'd known since childhood, frenzied in a religious fervor, turn on him and curse him, even do violence to him? Would his own father, if he were there, turn his back in disgust, allowing his impudent son to be scorned? Would he even join in, impelled by his faith, or his deeper fear of violating the allegiance of his baptismal vows, which obviated the otherwise impenetrable bonds of family?

He stands up quickly and walks out of the church. The storm has intensified and snow is falling in dark, swirling sheets, making it difficult to see. A fresh blanket of powder covers his car, and the ground glistens as though the earth has merged with the sky to form an unbroken crystal cloud. He steps cautiously, knowing the deceptive display is a mask concealing the slick ice underneath.

As he drives slowly down the mostly deserted road, he's preoccupied by the anxiety that almost overwhelmed him moments before. The feelings, *that* feeling: he understands he shouldn't have expected any comfort from visiting the church. It's too late for absolution, even if absolution was what he coveted. He has already tasted the fruits of free will and marveled as the world unfurled before him like an uncharted ocean. Yet all the while he sensed that austere, ancient face over his shoulder: in the classroom when his professors lectured, in the library while he immersed himself in a textbook, in the darkness as he explored the freshly discovered wonders of the female body. This distraction: was it the conscience operating, or the healthy heart resisting the lie? Freedom, he has begun to ascertain, comes at the expense of bludgeoning old, failed gods who, in the fullness of their powers successfully kept minds young and blissful. And ignorant. This is the ultimate faith one struggles with: faith in oneself.

Discussion: Faith (1)

*The Vision of Christ that thou dost see
Is my Vision's Greatest Enemy.*

I DIDN'T SAY that.
  But I'm happy to repeat it.

*When I was a child, I spake as a child, I understood as a
child, I thought as a child: but when I became a man,
I put away childish things.*

What he said.
God's will?
Who knows. I don't, but neither do you. No one can say except for the vulnerable ones who say it, and need to believe it in order to grant order or at least coherence to things that are, by any other measure, incomprehensible. Whether one is grappling with the death of a parent or contemplating the plight of impoverished people, there exists, in God, an easy, irresistible answer that removes doubt and eradicates responsibility (ours, His).

When we're young, or weak, or wanting, the concept of God is less a matter of belief than an enchanting vindication or our inability—or unwillingness—to confront our own fates.

We believe in one God,
The Father, the Almighty,
Maker of heaven and earth,
And of all that is, seen and unseen.

I *did* say that, often. Every week, in fact, from earliest memory through the summer after my senior year of high school. I was baptized and confirmed and served, without complaint, as an altar boy. All that time, I appreciated it and believed in it: the ritual, the words, and the ultimate reward that awaited all of us. My eventual self-imposed excommunication was neither rash nor uncomplicated. Like countless others born with a predetermined recipe for appraising this world, my dissatisfaction with—and ultimate disdain for—organized religion was a matter of considerable deliberation and more than a little disappointment.

He ascended into heaven
And is seated at the right hand of the Father.
He will come again in glory
To judge the living and the dead,
And his Kingdom will have no end.

December, 1989: I stopped midway through the familiar recitation and looked around me. Row after row of people—men, women, grandparents, children, some in Sunday best, others less formal—all reciting the lines in one undaunted voice, the voice of routine, history, and fidelity, some expressing a creed they felt articulated the core of our salvation—the fulcrum upon which our entire foundation, as fallible souls, is predicated upon—others repeating a memorized catechism, lines in the passionless play that was enacted each Sunday, some wholly invested, others indifferent, everyone endorsing this ceremony that preceded them and would, presumably, continue indefinitely after their deaths.

I closed my eyes and heard the words, trembling with revelation, albeit not the intended one that we're taught to aspire toward. For the first time this familiar oath, this fealty to an invisible force, seemed unsettling. It was, as I now understood it, the austere and unquestioning noise of a mob, however civilized. It occurred to me, egged on by the corrupting influence of Sociology and Psychology 101, that if I perceived this procession as one involving unclothed strangers chanting in an unfamiliar language, it would suddenly have more primitive connotations, or else invoke the brainwashed babbling of a cult. This sanctified service was different only because more people practiced it and it had been around longer—and was the one I'd been born into.

So what? Even if, reduced to its most simple origins, church served as a renunciation *(Because He is our God and we are his people and the sheep of His pasture...)*, and these solemn incantations were merely guidelines for the less discerning, so long as these performances were being directed, from above, by the author of this sacred text, why trouble oneself over aesthetic considerations?

We believe in one holy, catholic and apostolic church.
We acknowledge one baptism for the forgiveness of sin.
We look for the resurrection of the dead,
And the life of the world to come. Amen.

Here was the moment, the hackneyed shock of recognition, where you see something you've looked at a thousand times and it reveals itself, clearly. The response need not—or should not—necessarily lead to disenchantment or disbelief, but you have unwittingly opened a door that can't be closed. You can never not see things you've discerned, and you can't force yourself to forget them, although many people spend their lifetimes trying.

Whether it's a relationship, a job, or a religion, as soon as your participation seems pointless, or painful, or if it ceases to inspire you, it's time to look around—or better yet, inside—for other options. Some people need an answer; some people can never stop asking questions.

Maybe it was the drugs, the college curriculum, the embrace of free will as an agent of empowerment as opposed to a prison sentence, or the more (or less) complicated proposition that there was never any real possibility for me to emerge, as a semi-adjusted adult, reciting—much less accepting—the same magical thinking I was taught as a child.

Family History (2)
(2001, 1988, 1991)

THE HUSBAND LOOKS down at his wife and tries to count the number of times he has stood by her side in a hospital. The birth of their two children; her gall-bladder operation; the day she fainted after their son's tonsils were successfully removed, causing her to be briefly admitted herself; and then the surgeries and post-op stays dating back to August, 1997. A lot of times, he concludes. He doesn't want to think about how many times, in less than five years, he and his children have been obliged to sit—and sleep—in uncomfortable chairs while the woman they love suffered and recovered.

It's not time to think about it yet, he thinks. We're not ready to think about that (but it's out there to be thought about; everyone thinks about it, even in the abstract, even when they're healthy, even when there's no good reason to give those thoughts the time of day). He doesn't want to think about it, but sometimes the mind goes where it wants and there's not a whole hell of a lot you can do about it.

. . .

His father had gone first, which wasn't the way he'd anticipated it, as his father had been exceptionally, almost unusually healthy, unlike his mother. In retrospect, he'd come to understand that things had worked out for the best, as they usually tended to do. Had his father been left behind it would have been undesirable for all involved, not least his father. True, his father had an abundance of Irish vitality and an epic constitution, but his mother possessed the real strength.

It had been sudden—a phone call from one of his sisters. No time to prepare or react, only to process the news. *Daddy is dead.* There was an accident. Someone, another elderly man actually, had blown right through the red light, hitting his father in the crosswalk as he walked to the preschool to pick up his granddaughter, like he did every afternoon. *I never saw the light change*, the man tearfully claimed, repeating the apology over and over, the police officer reported.

Once the shock wore off, he found he felt more pity for the driver than for anyone else, even for his mother, who had her memories and her children. This man was unmarried, a blue-collar state employee afraid to retire, who would now live out his years knowing he'd taken another man's life. Whether he turned to the past or the future, he'd be equally trapped in either direction, asking himself, Why did this happen? How could this happen? The fact was, all of us have blasted past yellow lights, countless times, and any of those acts might have resulted in an accident that took some stranger's father, husband, or son.

His mother hung on for almost exactly three years. He was stunned how quickly the body will deteriorate once the will to live dissolves. He told himself during his father's funeral that while a sudden, unexpected death left the loved ones in a stupor, it was the best way for a person to go.

He had plenty of time to anticipate his mother's death, and began to prepare himself, instinctively, right after his father's funeral. There was no effective way to fortify oneself for the inevitable loss of one's parents. It wasn't something a healthy individual was disposed to linger upon. There was little comfort or insight to be gleaned from excessive introspection. It just finally, simply *happened.*

Near the end, when it became clear she wasn't leaving the hospital, he acknowledged he might not be by her side when she passed away.

He understood this was what he'd been spared by his father's abrupt death. And as pitiful as it would have been to endure, watching his father wither away would have been tolerable. The prospect of having to witness the will to fight ebbing from his mother's body inspired a fear that swelled against the foundation he had taken a lifetime to cultivate.

Another call, from his older sister this time: *They think she had a stroke.* Her health had been failing for the last few months, and it was obvious things were winding down. He spent three days at the hospital, flying up from Virginia, just as his wife had done a little over a decade before to be with her dying mother. He wasn't sure what to expect, but he needn't have worried. Nothing happened. His mother was mostly unconscious, preferable to being awake and suffering. But after three days it started to seem like she was defying him, testing his faith. He knew, on some level, that this was stress and lack of sleep. Still, he felt convinced she would continue to live so long as he stayed by her side. He asked himself two questions, over and over: How long should I stay? When was it enough? He and his older sister both lived in different states, with jobs and families to oversee. He resisted those awful but irrefutable words everyone uses before, during, and after another person's death: *Life goes on.* How long was one expected to wait?

No one else gave him the slightest pushback when he decided to return home. Call me if anything changes, he told his younger sister as he left the hospital. Getting in the elevator he felt a foreboding, and understood he should go back and look at his mother's face one last time.

Once again he needn't have worried; his mother hung on, in and out of consciousness for another month.

He was not by her side when she went. No one was; she passed away during the night, presumably already asleep. The last few months had not been easy, but in the final analysis, it was difficult to quibble (with God? Fate?) about how each of his parents had died. No prolonged or gratuitous agony, no spiritual torment that he was aware of. At least this is what he told himself; what he tried to believe.

Fathers and Sons (Truth)

(1988)

I DON'T BELIEVE what I just saw!

No one else in the room could believe it, either. Kirk Gibson had, before our eyes and on television, done something so improbable, so historical that we had no choice but to get drunk.

It was something we were developing the typical college freshman's proficiency for. I was getting good at a lot of things, not all of them necessarily good for me. I'd already become a professional at ordering pizzas late at night and passing out before I could eat them (the reason so many people of a certain age insist that pizza tastes better cold is because they have so much experience eating it that way; they have no other choice). It had only taken a few weeks of American History 101 to understand that maybe I should have been rooting for the Indians in all those old movies. I had discovered, with equal amounts of surprise and delight, that I was not in fact the only person in the world who still listened to bands like King Crimson, Jethro Tull, and Pink Floyd. I had overcome, with impressive ease, the initial guilt I'd felt regarding my official status as a contentedly lapsed Catholic: the more Sunday masses I missed, the less I missed the whole routine. The timing couldn't have been better, considering I had finally ended an eighteen-year sexual losing streak (Original Sin has no chance against unrestrained orgasms). I had been promoted to the Big Leagues and was doing everything I could to make sure they kept me around. I wanted to be a team player and I was pleased to establish that there was little I wouldn't do for the team: even if you lost the game it didn't matter as long as you left it all on the playing field, *et cetera*. The only thing, in short, that surprised me was how easily surprised I was at how little of life I had actually experienced thus far.

...

My parents hadn't had the privilege of hearing about most of these wonderful developments, in large part because I hadn't seen and had hardly spoken to them for half a semester. It wasn't personal, it was strictly business: I had things to discover and, being a team player, I certainly didn't want my parents wasting their money on my education.

But it had also been a less-than-peaceful transition, getting to this point. My folks had dealt better with the departure of my sister four years earlier, but at that time I was still around. In some ways, and for obvious and understandable reasons, I became closer to my parents while I was in high school. My relationship with my mother had invariably been present and positive, but it was during those awkward, impressionable mid-teen years that I became particularly close to my old man. Exhibit A: Rather than bemoaning my feeble inability to handle Algebra II, he took it upon himself to tutor me. Each night after dinner we would work through that day's assignment, and he displayed a patience and proficiency that I'd never witnessed or even imagined. I'd never had previous cause to doubt, for a single second, how much he cared about me, but it was during my junior year, when he

helped me fumble through a subject I would forget as soon as I got past it (which must have killed him, a man of math and science, seeing yet another child who possessed so little of his ability or interest in the very disciplines that gave his life purpose and passion), that I heard him say he loved me each night with actions, not words.

I wouldn't go so far as to imply that we became *friends* (although he seemed to understand, and appreciate—as a father and a man—the ways my mother and I had bonded over things he didn't share or espouse), but it was during this time that he became my *Pops*, and the real foundation, which we would require years later, was firmly established.

It was, then, startling and more than a little painful to witness him acting like such an insufferable prick as I left for college. During those weeks I saw a spiteful silence and intransigence I had never observed, not even during his sporadic periods of silent-treatment toward my mother when they fought.

What's your problem, I didn't ask, because I knew he had his reasons and therefore wouldn't be able to share them. Being a typically self-absorbed eighteen-year-old, it didn't fully occur to me that he was simply sad to see me go. I understood he wasn't *happy* to see me go, nor was I unequivocally happy to leave parents I genuinely loved, and more importantly *liked.* Having not dealt directly with absence or loss (excepting my grandmother, whom I'd been too young to properly mourn or miss), I was unable to fathom what my departure signified for my father, on theoretical as well as practical levels. He wasn't just watching his son depart (and apprehending, having been to college himself, the ways in which he was paying large amounts of money to ensure that I grew, changed, and figured out for myself all the ways I was unlikely to emulate him, philosophically as well as practically), he was being confronted with the unpreventable void of a house without children. If this was the first day of the rest of my life, it was the same, only more so, for him.

Still: to have the same man who had been to every single swim meet, soccer game, school function, and rite of passage giving me the cold shoulder was more than slightly disconcerting. Of course, I shouldn't have been surprised. Earlier that year I'd been in a car accident, during Christmas break, up in Boston. My cousin lost control and slid on black ice into a tree, which greedily ate the (fortunately for us, extensive) front end of the thrice-owned Pontiac he was driving. The injuries were minimal, although uncertainty remained about whether or not I'd broken some ribs. At the hospital they confirmed I had *badly bruised* them, which disappointed me because I wouldn't have as good a story to tell. By the time my old man arrived, he was his typically stoic self. "You clowns are lucky," he said, and I didn't disagree with him.

The next morning his father, Gramps, came in to check on me. "We're glad you're okay," he said, and I didn't disagree with him. "Now you know how Darrell Green feels after every Redskins game." He smiled, and then he got serious: "Your father was very upset when the hospital called. He was really shaken up until they confirmed you were all right." He said some other things, but I was still trying to imagine a scenario that could ever cause my father to become flustered to the extent that it was noticeable. For a teenager who figured he knew everything, this conversation was an invaluable opportunity to concede that all sorts of things happen that none of us necessarily see. I didn't need to see my father unnerved and scared on behalf of his son to appreciate how much he loved me, but I was also grateful my grandfather had revealed the way I would never otherwise hear him express, without words, the things he couldn't always bring himself to say.

...

My roommate came down the hall just as we were cracking open our first beers. He told me I had a phone call. I asked, "Who is it?" "I think it's your father," he said.

Fathers and Sons (Fiction)

(1991)

CLEANING OUT THE HOUSE was the most difficult part.

His mother's funeral had been in October; now it was Christmas week. The house was unoccupied for the first time in more than fifty years. Walking into an empty house would have been easier; it was unsettling to see all the furniture, associated with memories going back as far as he could make them, not serving any purpose except awaiting their final destination—repurposed or retired. All the older, used-up and unwanted artifacts would go to the dump. This was what they were here for. He knew this was not going to be easy, as it seemed they were at once attending to, and facilitating, the last rites of the house—a house that had surreptitiously assumed its own identify during the time it had served and sustained his family.

Immediately, and without warning, the father felt the perceptible weight of history shifting to his shoulders. *It's me now,* he thought with a sluggish panic. *I'm the one, the next in line.* He looked at his son and realized, not for the first time, that rites of passage did not present themselves when you were prepared for or amenable to them; they occurred according to whatever natural (or random) order they happened to follow. The family name, he thought. My son's the last one; it either continues or ends with him. And then, he's still a *kid*. There is plenty of time to think about that. There were more immediate concerns to attend to.

. . .

His son had been able to say it. The one thing he most wanted to hear; the thing he *needed* to hear, even if he was unable to articulate (or acknowledge) it until the second it was said—because it might not have been said.

"I'm here," his son said. "I'm not going anywhere."

They had looked out at the Boston skyline earlier that morning. Halfway up Blue Hills Reservation, *Big Blue*—the miniature mountain where they had hiked and had picnics for decades. They walked, then stood, then sat, mostly silent, not saying much as little needed to be said. They had gotten through the funeral, the first holidays, and now they had the rest of their lives to live. But first they had to clean out the house.

. . .

The attic had not been entered in who knew how long. The son had never been up here and the father had not seen the inside of it since well before his wedding. Years of dust and darkness seemed suspended in the air, a sentient presence ambivalent about being disrupted after so much time. The space was a personal museum of desks, drawers, papers, books, pictures, clothes, and bags, all long-since relegated to supporting roles, now artifacts of personal authenticity. Two iron bed frames seemed to have taken root in the wooden floor; a vintage Victrola in which mice once made a nest had transformed into a shapeless form of petrified neglect. A sealed box revealed outfits he and his sisters had worn as children. As he sorted through tiny pairs of white shoes and the old-fashioned dresses and suits, he looked up at his son, understanding that most of these articles he held were over fifty years old—more than two of his son's lifetimes.

He could feel the tears coming and he stared down at his hands. One drop clung to his eyelid, holding on for its life. Finally, reluctantly, he allowed himself to let it out. He saw his son watching him and before he could stop it, he heard himself speaking: My mother lived in this house for sixty years and then died, alone, in a hospital...

It's alright, Pop. We still have our family; we still have each other.

Yes, we do, he said, embracing his son, the boy who was not quite a man, but close enough. We have each other, and that's all that matters. I love you...

This is what he *wished* to say. It was what he could almost hear himself saying. But such things are seldom said between fathers and sons. Instead, he focused his eyes on his hands, and then the floor, slowly regaining his composure. He put the clothes back in the box and said nothing.

...

It took most of the afternoon before they had finally transported everything into the rented moving van. His parents, like so many who had lived through the Depression, were reluctant to discard almost anything. There will probably be some valuable antiques in that attic, his wife had predicted. Probably, but he didn't have any particular inclination to establish which items, blanketed in black soot, might have been worth something.

After the last load had been taken to the landfill—which swarmed with seagulls, obscenely out of place as they circled the mounds of trash, an ocean of sorrow—it seemed as though he held the last fragments of his family's story, the secrets of his childhood, in his hands. Throwing the boxes and bags into the larger piles of other boxes and other bags—the spoils of separate family's discarded goods and detritus—seemed like a sacrifice to the memories of our deceased: they were lost in one another, in *themselves*, absorbed into the moving stream of shared recollection, all mixed up and intermingled. Different, the same, ultimately dissipated in time.

Like our souls, he thought, looking at the discordant array of rubbish, dispersed like abandoned and broken down buildings. *Ashes to ashes, dust to dust.* Everything is accounted for, our bodies, our belongings, our souls. Heaven, Hell, Nowhere: a junkyard of expired souls. Unless, of course, there was a more profound, impenetrable plan, a purpose that obliterated or redeemed this cycle of despair. It was one or the other, either an infinite sanctuary or the emptiness of oblivion. He knew what he chose to believe; what he *needed* to believe.

. . .

Later, as they pulled out of the driveway, the father looked up at the house, scarcely visible in the frigid twilight. It stood, imperturbable, looking down at him like it always had. In its silence, it seemed to signal something that nobody but him could understand.

He forced himself to look back one last time as they drove away. The house appeared to have withdrawn into itself as though, with a resigned sigh, it had finally surrendered to a deep slumber.

Premonition

(2000)

She can't remember the last time she caught a cold.

This isn't to say she didn't catch them, or suffer from allergies, reflux, chronic lower back pains, frequent urinary tract infections, headaches, fatigue, anxiety, and depression. Rather, an ingrained reaction to any illness caused her immediately to consider her mother—her mother's symptoms, and her own symptoms less than three years earlier (her mother had persistent pain behind her eyes that became too intense to tolerate and by the time they saw a doctor it was too late; she herself came back from summer vacation in 1997 with stomach pain that became unbearable overnight, escalating the suspicion of food poisoning to appendicitis until a surgeon discovered a tumor undetected behind her appendix, like the moon being covered by a cloud).

Ever since her mother's death in 1980, a recurrent cough or soreness would open the almost infinite portal of possibility. Is *this* how it starts? Is this fever what I'll remember as the first symptom that set the final sickness in motion? Is this ache a calling card of damaged cells that returned from the wrong side of town bringing the worst kind of bad news?

She could no longer simply endure the routine bouts of bronchitis without contemplating the history of maladies ranging from the ordinary to the exotic. This is what her mother's death did to her. This is what her own recent scare—the symptoms, the surgery, the recovery, the prognosis—had done to her.

Until 1997 it was more indulgent, almost superstitious, like obsessing about whether or not she'd locked the door or turned off the iron even though she *knew* she had, the sort of compulsion that practice, and medication, had helped her control. Now the trauma of her operation had provided context, a foundation to validate, even provoke her phobias. She knew this could go nowhere good, but she also knew there was nowhere good cancer could go.

After 1997 she didn't need to feel any symptoms at all. At any time, all those images and memories might flash through her mind, capable of derailing—in an instant—the best day she might have been enjoying. Paranoia or a premonition? She couldn't know until she *knew*, and then, of course, it was too late. But even those thoughts were (mostly) manageable, understandable even. Who could blame her for thinking such thoughts? Not her doctors. Except that now she was dealing with a new type of dread and it tended to wait until the middle of the night. It would wake her from wherever she had been (the bliss or oblivion of her dreams) and the urgency of an unanswerable question would render her breathless, immobile in her bed: *What if it's still inside of me? What if it has already come back?*

Machinery (8)

(2000)

THE HARDCORE CHEMOTHERAPY commenced just as the sweltering summer of 2000 settled into its sustained, apathetic groove.

Our family took turns getting my mother to her appointments,
and while none of those occasions were pleasant, they were, for
the most part, predictable. We knew what to expect, she knew
what to expect, and we all regarded this series of treatments as a
high-percentage strategy for survival. There was no creeping pes-
simism or confusion: the stakes were clear and we all had reason
to imagine things might be better in the not-distant future.

As such, we adapted to our new routines and it wasn't so much
a matter of who did what, it was who could do whatever, whenever. That summer we were still on offense; we had hope to spare
and the unified sense of purpose any family requires to make it
through an ordeal. It was, in short, almost businesslike, each of us
doing what needed to be done. Since my mother was handling all
the dirty and difficult work, our mission was to elevate her spirits
any way we could.

We had a lot going for us. The surgery in March had been successful: another tumor (large but not too large) had been extracted.

This course of chemotherapy—aggressive and therefore excruciating—was undertaken with an expectation of winning the battle, not postponing or prolonging it. My sister's three-year-old daughter and baby boy provided amusement and distraction. We were still locked in on the present and not overly obsessed with the future; we had absorbed the various prognoses and possibilities and were on the same page about how to proceed.

Yes, you were almost in the clear, we would tell her, and each other.

Yes, the cancer did come back, but we knew that was always a possibility.

No, there's no reason to worry it will come back again. The surgery was successful, and this chemo should make sure it stays gone.

No, I don't think it will come back, we told her, and each other.

No, I don't know what to hope for or believe, none of us ever said out loud.

Machinery (4)

(2000)

THE PATIENTS SIT in a large room, stationed in reclining chairs and hooked up to machines slow-dripping destructive fluids into their bodies. The idea being: you fight fire with fire, don't negotiate with terrorists, break a few eggs to make an omelet, etc. Above all never let on how worried you actually are.

She always brought a pile of magazines with her. Books were too difficult these days; it was cumbersome to read line after line and keep track of page after page. After a while it made you aware that you were concentrating, and the only way to do anything that requires concentration is to forget you're capable of doing anything else. Magazines were good, since pictures broke up the action and helped the pages turn more quickly and easily.

Her son encouraged her to listen to music, but she didn't like having headphones on in a public place; it felt as though she might miss something. Even though the doctors made themselves scarce here, just like at the hospital, you never knew when one might appear, so you had to be prepared. Music was capable of pleasant distraction, but she needed to be in the right place and the proper state of mind. She still couldn't believe her son listened to music at all times and claimed he needed music on in order to fall asleep.

It was from college, he explained. Having roommates meant you either adapted to their schedules, or you trained yourself to study, relax, and even sleep with the accompaniment of music.

He made her tapes that he promised would help, but she couldn't listen to them here. Rather than soothing her, they caused her to consider the things she would rather ignore. For instance, the tubes sticking out of her body, the hypnotic pings from the plastic bag, the faded blue veins in both arms, the scuff marks on the tiled floor, the scattered chairs spread strategically around the room, the various brochures strewn across the tables, the other patients (of all ages, of course, but not children, thank God; she would not be able to handle that), the familiar looks on all their faces, even the ones fortunate enough to be able to sleep.

She could not sleep. Her anxiety was mostly under control, but not enough to help her forget where she was (even if she wanted to) and certainly not enough to enable her to sleep. She didn't savor any of this, but it was tolerable so far; she accepted that this was what it would take to ensure she could stay away from surgeries and checkups and future chemo infusions. Hopefully. Still, she envied the people who were able to displace all thoughts and nap until it was time to leave.

She did notice that most of the patients were unaccompanied. Her husband and son stayed with her when they could, but they also had their jobs to get back to. Her daughter stayed sometimes, but it was always difficult with the young children.

So she brought her magazines and she welcomed the company of her family whenever they were available. But mostly these hours were spent alone with her thoughts, without music and without the escape of sleep.

Adaptation

(1960s, 1980s)

REMEMBERING. EVERYTHING CHANGES after a baby is born. This is what everyone told her. Her mother had told her everything, but—she would come to understand—nothing can be said to fully prepare a woman for the ways her existence is altered. It wasn't until you left the hospital and realized you were alone that the surprising pleasure wore off and the fear set in.

It was, of course, more than the physical (and easily identifiable, easily explainable) symptoms contributing to the lethargy that led, at times, to despondency. Even during the times when she wasn't fearing the uncertain future, or lamenting an irretrievable past, she grappled with the reality that motherhood—being alone each day with a child—was capable of inducing frustration and anxiety she had never previously felt. She understood—and accepted—that her husband had to leave early each morning for the job that provided the immutable necessities of shelter, sustenance, and security. More, it was a job he enjoyed and excelled at; he was doing what he was supposed to do, and she couldn't object to that. She was nevertheless unable to entirely suppress resentment at being alone so much.

Housewife. The term too often uttered by men (and unwed women) with denigration, and ignorance. So what? Well, to acknowledge that the routine of feeding, cleaning, and tending to a baby could occasionally be tiresome to the point of exasperation was, in effect, to admit negligence, or defeat. It was all but impossible for a woman to express how terribly afraid, and even angry, she could become as she looked down helplessly at a child, unable to determine why it was screeching. The ceaseless concern for the welfare of the baby (who depended entirely upon you for its innocent life) was capable of provoking an agitation that seemed uncomfortably close to hysteria. Nothing could prepare a woman for this, and even a mother who was experiencing the dread and despair—and feelings of inadequacy—was usually at a loss to articulate her consternation. This is what she read. This is what she lived.

Postpartum depression. Her mother had experienced similar symptoms after the birth of her first child. *It's very common.* This is what the doctor told her. This is what her husband constantly reminded her. It was what she repeatedly said to herself. Unfortunately, to her way of thinking, this knowledge only amplified her distress. If she was back East, with familiar faces, with *family*, she was sure all this would be more tolerable. Being housebound, or in the slow process of physical recovery, would be a different proposition if her parents were there to take care of her, even as she tended to her newborn daughter. As it was, she was largely alone with her thoughts and feelings. And she occasionally caught herself entertaining irrational thoughts in her solitude that left her terrified. She was loath to admit, even to herself, that in flashes of frustration she visualized drastic and awful acts. She sometimes had to force away the maddening impulse to take her own life, or do harm to the tiny, trusting baby who lay before her. That she was even able to think such thoughts intensified her feelings of guilt and culpability. She began gradually to suspect the worst possible conclusion—that she wasn't a suitable wife, or mother.

...

I don't know if I can do it, she'd say to herself on the worst days. *How did this happen? How did I get here? Where am I going?*

"I don't know if I can do it," she said to her mother, again. Feeling guilty, again. Guilty about how she felt. Guilty about the long-distance charges. Guilty because she felt guilty.

"Of course you can," her mother said, again. "You're already doing it."

Her mother reminded her, again, how much help she had provided, being the oldest of seven. Her mother reminded her that every mother thinks similar thoughts, and that only the ones who genuinely question their abilities are fully engaged with what they're doing. Her mother reminded her it would get easier. It would get better. It would get enjoyable. Her mother told her that one day her own daughter would have kids and she would tell her the same things. Her mother promised her that they would laugh about this, often, as they each adjusted to their new roles once they added *grand* and *great* to the names their children's children called them.

...

Eventually, she no longer woke up crying each morning, and she made the gradual transition into comfortable—and confident—motherhood. It was during this time—the first year of her daughter's life—that she underwent the transfiguration from *young lady* to *woman.* She recognized and learned to celebrate this identity, her destiny. She was—and would be—a *housewife,* and after a while, even that once unbecoming designation was one she embraced, and endeavored to contend with, without reservation. It was, she realized, *her* house, the dinners prepared were *her* meals, and the personality that the apartment was to take on would be the reflection of *her* personality.

During these initial years of dedication and resolution, it never occurred to her in any direct or pressing fashion that a time would one day come when she'd cease to be a mother (at least in the same way she had been for the first two decades of her children's lives). This was not unnatural; her focus was not unlike her husband's, whose reality was in large part informed by his career. But just as an employee eventually becomes cognizant—on some level—that *retirement* is inevitable, if desired, a mother is understandably less inclined to envision how her primary role will one day be irrevocably altered.

And then, one day, your children have grown up and moved out of the house. Just as you can't imagine your life—and the ways it will change—before you have them, it's impossible to adequately prepare for how it will feel once they're gone. Of course they aren't *gone*, you remind yourself, even as you deal with your parents' mortality and your own, accepting that nothing lasts forever.

Of course she was happy—for them, for herself. She was also sad. She was even, if she could bring herself to admit it (and she could, on occasion), more than a little jealous. She could admit it; she wanted to admit it. She needed someone—besides her husband—to talk to, a role her mother, and increasingly, her children, had served. Someone to talk to about the things she could never talk to anyone else about. Of course they're still around, she reminded herself, but she needed to let them go just as she had once let them cry themselves to sleep. It was the ultimate act of love, allowing children to learn ways they can take care of themselves.

There were three pictures above the fireplace: her wedding, her daughter's wedding, and her son's high-school graduation. So many of her friends' marriages had ended in divorce, even the marriages she had admired and envied. So many of her friends' children required separate sets of photographs for special occasions. They had done it, she reminded herself. They lived up to every reasonable expectation, for their children, for themselves. This was a comfort, even if it also caused an indescribable sorrow at times. *Nothing lasts forever.*

There was a new question—once all the old questions had more or less been answered—that she couldn't help asking, even if she was uncertain how to answer it: *Now what?*

Machinery (5)

(2001)

THE SIGHTS AND SMELLS, never welcome, quickly become recurring, then established. Once you've patrolled the hallways of a recovery ward, or helped your mother to and from the bathroom when she can hardly walk—or stand—or changed her bandage after surgery (and seen the scar, like a breathing fissure that might open up and suck you in if you looked too long), you become mostly immune to the fluids and gases the body emits, the peculiar emanations that take on an artificial tinge in the too-cool air inside a hospital room.

You become accustomed to things you could not imagine for the simplest reasons: you have no choice. You slowly become attuned to the sights and smells of cancer. These are not confined to the places you go or the patients you help protect—they include what you detect around your house and inside yourself. You become philosophical by default, and find yourself thinking about how things used to be: a generation before, a century before, a millennium ago. You contemplate operations without anesthesia, or a time when operations weren't possible or even considered; if you suffered certain symptoms, you became expendable.

Natural law only became intolerable once our capacity to relieve—and understand—pain evolved with our brains and our contraptions. And you get perspective: it's better now than it's ever been, and that's all anyone living in the moment can reasonably ask for. This is progress: people used to die at home because they had to, because they had no say in the matter. Now, there are doctors who have been trained to treat you and there are few symptoms they can't find an explanation for. The things that used to kill us came to be treated by medicine that made us stronger.

We came to treat the body more like a machine than a soul covered with skin, and this is what saved us. As soon as we stopped soliciting the sky for answers—or assigning divine agents the acclaim for our survival—we started to consider the connected parts that make us all alike. We began to look inside, figuratively and then literally, and this is how the art of medicine was developed, and then refined to the point where any ailment seemed treatable, any death preventable. It's a tribute to our instinctual insistence on improvement that we won't tolerate explicable barriers if we can help it. Being human, we can contemplate our flaws and the ways to improve; we are also capable of acknowledging how far from the ideal we fall. In other words, we control what we can, and when we are unable to exert our will we make war (or peace) with our minds. *Mind over matter* is what we say when we can't say anything else; it is intended to inspire but it also is an illusion. Trying to control our minds is another matter altogether.

And sometimes it doesn't make a difference how compelling or rational your thoughts might be. Sometimes having perspective is not good enough when you're obliged to watch someone you love struggle with pain and fear—the two things that our minds and machines ultimately are powerless to protect us from.

You may find yourself an adult, keeping watch over a grown infant (who happens to be your mother) in a hospital room, who licks her dry and cracked lips. She would be salivating if she had any spit, craving the simple, now sublime pleasure of an ice chip. An ice chip that she isn't allowed to have; even this paltry, pathetic pleasure must be denied, for her own sake.

And you might think: Is *this* as far as we've come? Someday, hopefully in the foreseeable future, we'll look back on these ordeals and find them cruel yet amusing. After a procedure that removes a portion of a woman's guts, where she gets stapled together like a flesh textbook, after having a vacuum tube snaked through her nostrils to suction out the leftover mess in her stomach; after all this and being compelled to find solace with a prognosis of *maybe*, all she wants, all she can imagine (all she is reduced to craving?) is a tiny chunk of frozen water. And she isn't allowed to have it.

We worked shifts to ensure she was never alone. Even when she was asleep. Especially when she was asleep, because that was when the staff expected patients to sleep, and if you couldn't, you were on your own. (This isn't an indictment of the nurses, already overworked and tasked with too many patients to keep up with even in ideal circumstances—and conditions in any hospital, practically by default, are never ideal.)

The anesthesia mixed with the meds occasionally caused a curious fugue state that made her at once childlike yet frail like an older woman. Under almost any other circumstances this could have been somewhat cute and endearing, but there's nothing cute or endearing about watching your mother toss and turn, speaking to people who aren't there and seeing things no one else can see. After a while, as you sit with her in the darkness, it occurs to you that she may know exactly who she's seeing and what she's saying.

Machinery (∂)

(1980)

SHE SITS IN the hospital room.

She looks at her father.

She looks down at her mother.

Is this what you'll be like, when I see you in heaven, or wherever it is we go? Or will you appear to me as you did on my wedding day? Will I weep again with joy when you smile at me? Will our loved ones be gathered around us? Will you be older? Will you be what you are right now, this husk of bones? (No!) Will you somehow be all of these things, as you are even now in my mind? How will we give and receive love? Will I recognize you at all?

She hears the priest's voice, speaking at her daughter's baptism. *We are all equals in the eyes of God.* Yes. *We are all created in the image of our Father.* No. *I want to know you and recognize you. I don't want to forget these things.*

She reaches down for her rosary beads. She looks back at her mother, supine and stationary. Suddenly the practical, practiced faith and belief in the goodness of human beings that has stood her through every test—her ability to love a salve against the iniquities and injustices of this life, the solicitudes of raising her own children, the faith that has made her life meaningful, the conviction that she understands what caring entails—is revealing itself, abandoning her in the eyes of the mother she loves, whose life is slipping away. Her faith has always comforted her, giving courage and belief. Now, for the first time, it occurs to her that faith will not be enough because it's all for naught if nothing else remains. Anything but nothingness, she thinks. Just darkness and nothingness, not *that*...

Is she trying to move?

She watches her mother's eyes become still and focused as she shifts slightly, a shadow beneath the sagging sheets.

Is she trying to speak? Is she praying?

"We're here...can you see us?"

Her lips move but no sound comes out.

She looks eagerly at her mother's face, as though in that moment it might still be possible to will her to rise. To help her stand beside the bed so she can tell them everything will be all right, as she always has. To help them believe.

Then, suddenly, she realizes: *She's waiting for us to say it's okay.*

"It's okay," her father is saying. "We're okay, you can go..."

Her mother opens her eyes and looks up, as if trying to communicate something she's already seeing. The eyes close, open, and then—still.

She looks into those eyes and then, in spite of herself, she finds herself looking upward, expecting to see her mother. Not the pale, lifeless shell on the bed, the *real* presence, ascending up and out of the room, a shimmering trail reflected in the sun's light like stained glass, consoling them all one last time.

The Abandoned Baby

(1967)

NEVER FORGET THIS feeling. She would never allow herself to forget the abandoned baby; she never wanted to forget him. She still saw that baby, all these years later, mostly when she was asleep. Kind of like a movie, a work in progress, a motion picture in the mind. Memories can refract reality, where we see what we've done, or what we wished we'd done, or what we might have done, what we should not have done, what someone else may or may not have done, and what we may or may not have done if we were someone else. Mostly, we see things we don't want to see, the things we try not to allow ourselves to see.

...

At that time there had been a substantial Native American population in Flagstaff, although it was congregated on (or relegated to, to be accurate) the outskirts of the city—on the border of the arid expanse of the desert. The conditions in which these people were obliged to exist were unacceptable, unconscionable. She had certainly seen some of the more unsavory areas of Boston (back when they didn't call them slums) and she had been to New York City. She also watched the news, which—to anyone with eyes half-open—adequately conveyed the realities too many people were accustomed to. But no urban experience could have prepared her for the squalor the Indians (as they were called back then) had to endure. She found it almost impossible to believe that in *this* country, in *this* day and age, a community (any community) was without running water or indoor plumbing. If these circumstances represented more than a passing concern among the middle-class citizens of Flagstaff, she wasn't aware of it. It seemed to be a situation, disgraceful as it was, that folks were able—and willing—to ignore, as if the mere mention of *those* people would initiate a conversation, or stir some semblance of recognition.

They'd spent their daughter's first birthday in the hospital after she developed a fever that didn't break for two days. She had her own room, a consideration that seemed automatic, nonnegotiable. During the times they weren't allowed in their daughter's room they went to the cafeteria, or while her husband busied himself with the magazines in the waiting room, she paced around, nervous and unsettled. Seeking an uncomplicated distraction she had walked up to the glass window and looked down at the newly delivered babies. Half the cribs contained infants who were carefully identified by name, weight, and time of birth. The remaining cribs were empty except for the one on the end, which held a boy who looked as old, if not slightly older than her daughter. She walked along the glass to get a better look, and when she stood directly in front of the crib she saw it was an Indian baby. His face confirmed that he was older than her daughter, but his body was frail and filthy. The little boy was obviously emaciated from ill-health or lack of nourishment; likely both. His hair was long and matted to his forehead and looked as if it had been dirty for an extended time. When he turned on his side she could see the dirt encrusted in his fingernails and a rash of red spots scattered across his back.

She was almost overwhelmed with a compulsion to demand that the boy be properly attended to. She even entertained the idea of snatching him and taking him home. She had seen plenty of movies. She also knew, at once, that this scenario, however well-intended, was impossible.

. . .

As they drove home the next evening with their daughter, she mentioned the Indian baby to her husband; she had to talk about it. Probably abandoned, he said, shaking his head. That happens a lot more than we realize. But couldn't the parents, or *someone* at least visit him? How could anyone just leave a child there, alone, staring at the wall like that with dirt on his face? I don't know, he replied. This kind of thing happens all over the world, all the time. It's unacceptable, she persisted. Well, the fact of the matter is, there's probably one poor kid like that in every hospital in the country, maybe more. And those are the ones fortunate enough to make it to a hospital. I don't want to talk about it anymore, she said, turning to make sure their daughter was secure in her car seat.

Her husband had been able to explain it, or at least rationalize it, intellectually. She knew it appalled him as well, but he was able to acknowledge it and move on, like everyone had to do unless they had no choice. Unless they were driven to distraction, without a way to tune it out, eventually overcome by the immensity of it. Or else they found the courage of their convictions and did something, anything. Gave it all away and did what Christ instructed his followers to do. *Go and sell what thou hast, and give to the poor, and thou shalt have treasure in heaven: and come and follow me.*

She understood this and she believed in this, but she knew she couldn't do it. Yes, she would never forget that unfortunate baby, and the millions like him. She would sponsor foster children for the rest of her life. She would dream about this baby, who seemed to incorporate all the sorrow and suffering of this world. She would see him in the streets when she drove past a huddled mass barely breathing beneath its blankets. She would wake up in tears, wondering if this cognizance was a direct call from God, the ultimate test of faith that so many of us necessarily fail. And she would think of her own family, and all she'd been spared, and find solace in the work she could do for her own children. It was a start; it was something. And most of the time it was enough; mostly she understood that if God created sadness He also orchestrated joy, and how could she be culpable for the grim laws put in place centuries before she became aware of them? Mostly she understood that no resolution, no answers, no contrition could quell the misgivings or provide catharsis. And so she grappled with these feelings as best she could, feelings that left her in an irreconcilable place where she remained alone and unconsoled.

Mothers and Sons (Truth)

(2001)

THE ROOM WAS DIM and cool, a shadowy contrast to the searing humidity outside.

Her son had left his car running while he took her upstairs. In the elevator she noticed he'd sweated through his shirt and she felt guilty, once again. He had to get back to work, having left to drive her here, like he'd done so many times this summer, like her husband had done and her daughter as well. Thank God he worked close by; thank God he *lived* close by. Thank God both her children were close and involved; there was no chance she could get through this without them, no chance her husband could bear this burden by himself. She knew, even as difficult as everything had become, that she was fortunate.

She thought about her mother and how quickly everything had happened. They hadn't caught it in time; less than four months from diagnosis to death. Something else to feel fortunate about—at least they caught this the first time, then the second, and again. *At least this gives you a chance, at least you can hold on to hope.* She had kept her capacity for hope alive when her mother got sick. And then she saw her. Living in another state (something she couldn't help; something she'd never been able to fully reconcile), she'd heard the updates and listened to her mother's voice on the phone. It wasn't until she saw her that she knew. Worse, her mother knew she knew, and then *she* knew. It was summer then, as well—stifling, unforgivable. Those handful of months measured by hope, expectation, and finally acceptance. It was over so quickly nobody had time to make adjustments or contemplate alternatives. For her, it was a summer of silence. She had nobody who could comfort her (that was what her mother did) and nobody to whom she could talk. She talked to God but it was a one-way conversation. Still, she prayed, she hoped, and she tried not to believe the things she saw when she was alone and it was silent.

She sensed she was being watched.

She looked over and the woman was indeed scrutinizing her, an elderly woman who'd been sitting alone when she'd arrived. She started to look back at her magazine and felt guilty, again. She could feel those eyes measuring her, craving reciprocation.

"Hi," she said, smiling.

"Hello," the woman responded, a bit startled, maybe unaware that she'd been staring.

She smiled and looked back at her magazine.

"Hot out there, isn't it?" the woman said.

"I'm sorry?"

"I said it sure is hot out there, isn't it?"

"Oh, yes. Very hot."

"Hot as blazes," the woman said.

"On our way over the car said it was ninety-five, and that's without the humidity!"

"Was that your son who was here before?"

"Yes, he and my daughter help my husband get me to my appointments."

"My husband passed away two years ago," the woman said.

She went on to say several more things. After a while, she asked a question that didn't require a response because both of them understood she already knew the answer. It sounded like a question but it was actually a statement, a reminder for anyone who would listen. It was the simple truth the woman confronted every day that she needed to share with someone, to make sure someone else knew. She was still alive—and she was alone.

Mothers and Sons (Fiction)

(2001)

AGAINST ALL PROBABILITY, it seems to have gotten even hotter outside. As he walks out to the car, his eyes take several seconds to adjust to the glare of the sun. His body, numbed by the cold air inside, now comes alive and quickens under the moving waves of heat.

He drives down familiar roads, sufficiently distracted by unfamiliar thoughts that he almost fails to notice the figure standing in the middle of the intersection. He reaches for his horn, more instinct than anger, then realizes it's an elderly woman. He slowly pulls up next to her, rolls down his window, and speaks.

"Hi. Is everything okay? Are you all right?"

The woman, either unconcerned by or oblivious to the fact that she's stopped in front of oncoming traffic, shrugs.

"Can I help you? Would you like a ride home?"

She looks at him hesitantly, then smiles, equal parts relief and gratitude. "Yes, thank you…that would be nice."

He jumps out of the car and opens the door for her.

"I live in the Fellowship House," she says, easing into her seat. "It's only a mile or so away…"

"Sure, that's no problem," he replies, dumbfounded that the woman has walked anywhere at all in this weather.

"This heat, I think we might break some records today," she says. "It's already above ninety, and that's without the humidity."

He turns the radio off and drives slowly down the road. After a minute or two of uncomfortable silence, he says the first thing that comes into his mind. "People die in this weather, you know. It happens all the time, and then you read about it in the newspapers."

The woman says nothing at first. "Well, you're so young. God bless your youth, I'll tell you."

Again unable to catch himself, he says, "I guess you never appreciate what you have until it's gone." Silently he curses his stupidity.

The woman nods. "I know what you mean and it's true."

He laughs nervously. He's aware of his own vitality, making her frailty seem so foreign, so frightening.

You never appreciate what you have until it's gone.

He starts, unsure if he's spoken aloud. The woman gives no indication either way, smiling at him with a maternal expression that suggests a lifetime of concerns and troubles, interests and solicitudes. Their eyes meet. The woman possesses a dignity that belies her infirmity. She's on her own but she's not helpless.

I am still alive, the eyes tell him.

He feels a peculiar compulsion to confide in her, as thought it might somehow make amends for the disparity that so glaringly divides them. As he flounders for appropriate words, the woman speaks of the one thing he realizes (too late) he doesn't want to hear.

"The people at the Fellowship House are very nice. They take good care of us there."

He says nothing, uncomfortable with the silence that now fills the car. His head feels heavy and he envisions the environment this woman lives in, the stifling conditions that confine her, giving regimented meaning to her identical days.

"You remind me of my son," the woman says after a while.

He smiles politely.

"Although he's older...how old are you?"

He lies.

"Yes, he's older, but he's still very handsome. And he has a wonderful wife."

He nods, making a concerted effort to keep his eyes on the road.

"I'm very proud of him, as I'm sure your parents are of you."

He nods again, watching the yellow lines flash past his tires. He can sense the woman watching him.

"My husband passed away two years ago," she says.

"I'm very sorry to hear that."

"And my son sold our house. He wanted to put me in this place, the Fellowship House, after my husband died. I told him I'd rather stay in my own house..."

He looks over quickly and it occurs to him that he may be the first person outside the cautiously constructed world of doctors, orderlies, and senior citizens to whom this woman has spoken in a long time.

"...but he said this was the best thing," she continues. "So we sold the house."

He listens helplessly and wishes he hadn't offered the woman a ride. And then he feels guilty. He wipes the single drop of sweat that flashes across his forehead, smiling and nodding although he doesn't hear what the woman is saying. He tries to suppress a surge of unease unlike anything he's ever experienced. He hears, or rather senses, that the woman continues to speak, and he's vaguely aware that he also is talking, but he doesn't know what he's saying. He attempts with great difficulty to concentrate on the road and speak at the same time. His movements are torpid and his mind, which has been racing, slows to the point that it seems—for a moment—that the woman is speaking clearly and quickly, that she's the much younger one. He forces himself to keep his eyes directly on the road; he's desperately afraid to look at the woman so he looks up, ahead, and sees the top of the Fellowship House through the trees. In that moment the disorienting sense of recognition falls away and relief surges through his clear mind.

"…so I came here, alone," the woman continues.

Almost alone, he thinks.

"My son said as soon as they bought the new house and settled in he would come and get me."

He pulls up in front of the tall brick building and stops the car.

"That was two years ago," the woman says quietly.

She starts to reach for the door and then speaks, almost to herself.

"Do you think he's ever going to come?"

He meets her gaze and blinks as another drop of sweat falls into his eye.

"Of course he is," he says, and tries another smile. The woman seems to sense his effort.

"Thank you for the ride," she says and slowly lets herself out of the car.

He watches the woman walk through the revolving door without looking back.

He drives off quickly, feeling sick and eager to escape. As he reaches down to turn on the radio he catches a glimpse of his face in the mirror and abruptly looks away.

He understands that the woman has been telling him about himself.

Discursion: Faith (2)

I SEE THE woman, sitting silent, alone, waiting for the bus that may or may not decide to pick her up today.

I think: same woman, same bus stop, same book in her hands. Where is she going? What is she doing? What is she reading?

The woman is a nun, as her quaint costume makes abundantly clear. She sits alone, silent, a human statue: perfect posture now habitual from years of training, browbeating, and, ultimately, ardent emulation. Her attention to the small book she holds is entire, unyielding.

And it takes several seconds for the understanding to occur: this is a cliché. Of course. But like any cliché worth its stench, there is a twist, a discernible fork in the future, a possibility.

Either: this woman—this quiet, meekly loyal, unreservedly religious woman—is, of course, reading the bible. For the thousandth time, the millionth? In her unremarkable way fortifying one of the increasingly intractable truths: the possibility still exists that custom and tradition count for something, are still worth attaining. And this woman, this archetype, beautifies what should not change, an innocence somehow not contaminated by our co-opted culture.

Or: it brings into sharp relief the pitiful, ceaseless certainty that our capacity for wonderment, our curiosity and confusion, are not strong enough to escape superstitions and easy answers: that anyone could find comfort, or meaning, in a ritualized routine, reading the same spurious words endlessly, unfolding their anti-mysteries into eternity.

About Miracles

(July, 2002)

i.

BELIEVING IN MIRACLES requires faith. Faith in miracles, faith in *faith*.

The bible, taken on faith, is God's Word and the document of His work. Miracles are, for the faithful, not merely possible or even expected, but inevitable. Blood into wine. Eyesight to the blind. Conception and then ascension, beyond and back into the skies. Death into life, eternal life after we die. With faith all things are conceivable.

ii.

One becomes wary of miracles the same way—and for the same reasons—one disdains forced faith. After seeing a magician reveal his tricks, whether he's wearing a black cape or a white collar, the spell can never again be unbroken.

One conditions oneself to put away childish, or unreasonable things: one learns not to pray for miracles, to neither count on nor believe them. It has less to do with forsaking faith in the possible and more to do with reconciling oneself with what's not possible.

iii.

We found ourselves in need of a miracle. July, 2002: fourth time would not be the charm, we knew that going in.

The summer had started badly. When my father called Memorial Day and said he and my mother could not make the family picnic, I knew. *She isn't feeling well,* he told me, and I knew. It wasn't the resigned tone of his voice, or the abruptness of his announcement (she'd been doing so well...); it was a feeling, somewhere between my gut and my brain, that told me we had dodged too many bullets, had too many strikes called balls, gotten out of too many traffic tickets, as well as other clichés I hadn't considered. I just *knew,* the way I hadn't known in '97 (none of us did) or in 2000 (none of us allowed ourselves) or in 2001 (I can only account for myself here). I knew.

Things got worse in a hurry, because with cancer once things get really bad they stay bad. A little less than halfway through the summer we brought her in for what we suspected would be the final surgery. The big question this time was not whether they could save her, or what they would find, but if they could even do anything once they got in there. *We won't know until they get inside,* we told ourselves, a shard of hope, a last fortress against fate.

. . .

The worst moments, of course, occur in the waiting room. It's unconscionable the way families are obliged to receive the news, good or bad, in front of each other: that negative diagnosis a public spectacle hardly tolerable for loved ones, much less strangers; a positive diagnosis a slap in the face of those anxious and suffering within earshot. In '97 the news had been unexpected—and not good—but they caught it *(They got it!),* so the shock was mitigated by how much worse it *could* have been *(She's going to make it!).*

2000 was the same scene, only more so. 2001 was disconcerting, a surprise *(It's back)* coupled with an inconclusive report *(We can't get rid of it all)*. We absorbed this verdict in the crowded space where everyone else sits and waits, a nerve-wracking purgatory we pay to provide (and, if possible, avoid).

"I'm going to the chapel," my father announced, and I followed him. "You don't have to come with me," he said, almost gently. It was the first time I'd seen him this close to defeat, the first time I'd noticed the thinnest red streaks on either side of his mouth—burst blood vessels from clenching his jaw so long and so hard. "No, I'll go with you," I said. It was the first time I'd ever voluntarily accompanied him to a place where you pray for things.

I sat while he knelt. I put a hand on his shoulder and we each thought our own thoughts. And even here, in this poor approximation of the churches we'd always attended, even as matters of life and death were being decided all around me, that familiar voice could not keep quiet. That voice inherited as birthright by anyone born into a family of faith, the conscience inside and beneath the sense of right and wrong, somewhere between my gut and my memory, the voice that sustains itself by feeding on fear and fantasy: *Maybe if you believed it would work.* Maybe, I thought, looking at my old man, his eyes squeezed shut and his mouth mumbling words I didn't need to hear. Maybe if we all believed nothing bad would ever happen, the troubles we cause could be more easily explained. Maybe if nothing bad ever happened we wouldn't need to believe. Maybe if we didn't believe we would never inculcate this formula that can make a human being like myself, at his most frail and vulnerable, capable of entertaining thoughts like this.

In July of 2002 we sat in or near the same seats where we'd sat so many times before, covered on all sides by people in similar boats, lost in magazines, conversations, fervent attempts to keep the worst fears in check. We were unflappable, for the most part: we'd been here too often and expected too little to put too much on the line. We were waiting to hear words like *stable, sustained,* and *second opinion.* We'd also seen too much to count on anything half as good as we'd heard during our last visits, however awful some of those things actually were.

I saw them first. They didn't see me. I had walked toward the lobby, pacing as the wait stacked one interminable minute on top of the next, each one infinitely more excruciating, offering an endless menu of possibilities and horrors. It's interesting the way we feel compelled to move in order to quiet our minds: sitting still makes us defenseless against an onslaught of unwelcome thoughts; pacing around provides distraction, however weak and fleeting. I saw the surgeon, accompanied by the oncologist, striding down the long hallway, coming toward us to tell us our fortune. I saw them and experienced a sensation, somewhere between my gut and my heart, that I hadn't felt in so long. It was the feeling of Hope fulfilled: the presents under the tree, the last day of class, the first drive in a new car. They didn't see me, and I saw something I couldn't believe. They were laughing. I saw them laughing and in that instant I understood. *It's a miracle!*

And I didn't renounce my faithless ways. I didn't make immediate bargains with dead people. I didn't feel the warm glow of divine intervention. I didn't see God's face in the empty spaces above me. My reaction was at once more simple and profound than that. I thought, *It's a miracle.*

I thought: They're laughing which is unbelievable which means it's good news which means something good happened and Mom's okay and it's a miracle and everything's under control and they can't believe it but this is the way it is and it's such amazing news because this never happens but that's why we never say we know until we know because we never know until we see with our own eyes and that's the only way we know for sure...

And then I watched them transform into the people I had known all along. As they walked closer, still not looking up to see me, I saw them slip back into character. I saw them assume the detached air of authority, exuding the aloof ambivalence that preempted accountability. I saw my mother's life flash before my eyes and the sinking feeling of the ultimate betrayal. They were no longer laughing and I watched, somewhere between what my eyes saw and what my mind imagined, a future that held things I had not, until this second, allowed myself to entertain.

They walked down the hallway and entered the waiting room, and I followed, and my father and sister stood on either side of me. Unsmiling, they delivered the grim news, their voices conveying the austere lack of identification they required in order to perform their roles as sometimes saviors.

Discursion: Faith (8)

You don't lose faith (and here I mean/refer to Faith with a capital F, or maybe that should be faith with a lowercase f—whichever kind we can associate with feelings not involving supernatural entities—the bigger kind, or smaller, depending on where you stand on such matters).

When you lose a loved one or something indelible happens to shake your balance or even shatter your belief that there's anything sensible about this life, you eventually come to a place where the one remaining issue is the only one you can't avoid or get around, and it turns out to be the thing that saves you. You're still alive, you're still around to try and make sense of it. Or, short of that, to keep drawing breath and taking more out of existence than it takes out of you. Just *being* is winning in the existential sense, no matter how cynical or nihilistic one feels about such matters.

Only until it happens to you, until you get your own death sentence (or, if you're lucky—or unlucky, depending on where you stand on such matters—you die suddenly and unexpectedly); only when your own light is about to be extinguished (forever or temporarily, depending on where you stand on such matters) do you have to confront whether or not you still have faith in how your life has played out.

In my case, my mother's death didn't shatter my faith; I'd already taken care of that matter on my own.

Rebellion

(2000)

i.

QUESTION: WHAT ARE you rebelling against?

Answer: Whaddya got?

The thing most adjusted adults eventually understand is that everyone who marches to that proverbial different beat does so not necessarily out of abandon or indifference; it's usually a calculated, even cultivated design for defiance. Of course, when you're young you have your youth to burn, like Marlon Brando on a motorcycle. Or perhaps you long to improve upon the petulance of previous generations: you hear the different drummer and then refuse to march even to that music. It isn't that you're going nowhere; you're content to not even go there, to keep one step ahead of oblivion, and achieve it by any means necessary so long as you're still inside the cyclone.

ii.

You think: *Sometimes it's better not to think.*

Ignorance, after all, is bliss and a little ignorance goes a long way, especially in this hyperspace, computer-chip, information-overload moment in time. A moment in perpetual fast-forward.

Time, it seems, can scarcely keep up with itself.

On occasion (every day, more or less), you find yourself overwhelmed by a compulsion to comprehend the things you can't control that have complete control over you. Things like aging and illness and quantum space and the mysteries of compassion. For starters. The things only poets understand, and who understands poets? Each person, it seems, must ultimately develop a progressive inability to understand the world in which he suffers and survives. And maybe this is a good thing, all things considered. Maybe this is for the best. If the necessary miracles of evolution unfolded in ways we could readily fathom, anarchy would likely ensue. If people understood how Nature really works and the ways in which the game is rigged, think of all the would-be Robinson Crusoes, setting sail for the deserted islands that no longer exist. They simply aren't *there.*

The future, as it always seems to be, remains at once exciting and intimidating to consider. And yet: thinking about the reality, the inevitability of the twenty-first century, it doesn't seem altogether possible. Can't we just slow things down a bit and grapple with the century that we let get away from us sometime back in the mid-to-late 1800s? The Pony Express, the phone, the phonograph, pasteurization, planes, product assembly lines, atomic bombs, apartheid, *All The President's Men,* politics as usual. Prosperity. Privation. Privacy. The Internet. Enough.

After a century of explosions—overpopulation, death, wealth, squalor, apathy, ethnic cleansing, email—is there anything left to establish or invent? Haven't we already outdone ourselves? What does the new century, the future, have to dole out that we haven't already discovered? What do we have to fear that doesn't already stare us dead in the face? Aside from the fact that we're still unable to cure ancient diseases, we can't feed everyone, superstitious tribes are ceaselessly quarreling, and every single one of us will eventually, inevitably die.

To be continued.

You think.

iii.

Milan Kundera, in the book *Testaments Betrayed,* explains his vision of the novelist's acumen, which is "a considered, stubborn, furious nonidentification, conceived not as evasion or passivity but as resistance, defiance, rebellion."

In *The Brothers Karamazov,* in the chapter entitled "Rebellion," the mercurial Ivan lays out his rationale for rejecting God. If the ostensibly benevolent—and omnipotent—Being who created us in His image can be credited for everything we see and achieve, He must also be accountable for all the inexplicable misery. Ivan is, ultimately, less concerned with Heaven or Hell than what occurs on God's watch, here on earth. Even if his personal salvation were secured, even if every soul's redemption was guaranteed, the arrangement is intolerable if it depends upon one innocent child being forced to suffer. Ivan is incapable of accepting any circumstance where ultimate peace is contingent upon anyone's pain. This is his rebellion.

Taking this scenario one step further, Ursula K. Le Guin, in her short story "The Ones Who Walk Away from Omelas," synthesizes elements of what both Kundera and Dostoyevsky are describing. In her tale, once certain types of people ascertain the way things really work (on earth as it is in heaven), they turn their backs and forsake the security of organized society. Unable to reconcile the cost of a not-so-ignorant bliss, Le Guin's heroes rebel by refusing to endorse—or even abide—the practical and spiritual cost of doing business.

In *Slaughterhouse Five,* Kurt Vonnegut draws an intractable line in the sand (or salt), siding with vulnerable humans over an infallible God: "And Lot's wife, of course, was told not to look back where all those people and their homes had been. But she *did* look back, and I love her for that, because it was so human."

iv.

Once I'd dispensed with organized religion and then determined that academia was no longer a suitable solution, I might have become paralyzed, either because of other options or the lack thereof. Instead, I felt oddly liberated, although that realization by no means occurred overnight. Eventually, I found I wasn't running away from anything so much as feeling compelled to run toward almost everything. Avoiding quiet desperation became my approach; finding ways to make art into life and life into art was my new mantra. (So simple, so impossible.)

My rebellion, if it could accurately (or fairly) be described as such, was rather simply an antagonism against cliché: clichéd thoughts, actions, excuses, and even intentions. I still wasn't certain what was going to work for me, but I was steadily recognizing what wasn't going to work. Understanding that bills had to be paid, relationships had to be cultivated, mistakes had to be made, and, above all, that one day I would no longer be around, my objective revolved around an obsession to live a life nobody but I could live. During those post-graduate years I steadily fortified, for all time, the most important—and rewarding—relationship of my life: the one with myself.

Discussion: Violence

i.

FIGHTING DOESN'T SOLVE anything. Everyone knows that. But then, the point of fighting isn't usually to solve anything, it's to settle something. There's a significant discrepancy between the two; ask anyone who used to (or still does) get into fist fights.

I was never that guy. Certainly I had some schoolyard scraps, but those were more wrestling matches at recess and I was semi-retired by fifth grade. I don't believe I've thrown or received a punch since I entered middle school. It had a lot to do with self-awareness: I knew I was not a fighter, did not relish the idea of getting into fights, and did not particularly enjoy witnessing them.

I can't overlook the role my mother played in the development of this penchant for diplomacy. Like most women, and mothers, she had an innate revulsion for cruelty and injustice. But more, she simply detested violence in all forms, the way most sensitive, evolved individuals do. Being a boy I did not, and do not, necessarily share that stance, or I do with some reservations. Hence my tolerance for—and, occasionally, appreciation of—realistic portrayals of mayhem in movies, or the otherwise indefensible spectacle of grown men trading punches in hockey games. But I did inherit an inability to comprehend brutality for its own sake, or the notion of deriving pleasure from someone else's pain. Of course there's considerable ground between behavior most rational people abhor and activities (like fighting) that some people can rationalize and even celebrate.

Toward the end of S.E. Hinton's book *Rumble Fish* the doomed older brother—a street legend who, like all tragic figures, sees everything clearly after it's already too late—looks at the Siamese fighting fish and suggests that their violence is territorial, not instinctual. If they existed out in the river, they wouldn't fight. This may or may not be true, but it's an allegory for gang violence, which is nothing if not a territorial battle.

It also, of course, speaks to the larger theme of violence being—among many other things—a consequence of timing, luck, and location. My old man grew up outside of Boston, and all of my extended family still lives less than a half hour from the city. It was, and remains, a very blue-collar, ethnic environment. As such, inadequate if revealing descriptors like *old school, tough,* and *real* were, and are, invoked. Even though genetics made me inclined to determine that the pen is mightier than the sword, if I'd grown up in the same neighborhood as my father, there are ways I would be different. Too many ways to count, certainly. I believe it's entirely possible I may have turned out much the same as I am today, but I'm also positive circumstances would have ensured that I was harder, less reflective, and more resilient. Put another way, the fact that I can even formulate such a hypothesis tends to bolster this theory, and I was taught—and trained myself—to use my mind instead of my muscle, not as a calculated choice so much as an inevitable outcome of my upbringing. Mostly, I remain grateful I had the opportunity to succeed (and be allowed to succeed) without the old-fashioned type of problem solving that impedes a healthier assimilation.

ii.

Writing is fighting, and few writers used their skills with as much focused indignation as George Orwell.

Orwell embodies an era when exploration (physical and intellectual), engagement with the world, and an insatiable appetite for experience were not rites of passage so much as imperative points of departure. Of course it was, in many regards, a simpler time: no movie stars or radio-friendly pop singers (no radio, for that matter), no prime-time news anchors sensationalizing the story of the day. To a certain extent, we counted on our writers (think Twain or Sinclair, or Dickens) to give us an unvarnished view of what was happening, hidden in plain sight.

In his harrowing essay "How the Poor Die," George Orwell describes his unexpected—and unpleasant—time at a nonpaying hospital in Paris. It's a typically instructive discursion on the issues that obsessed Orwell, and about which he wrote with more clarity than anyone else in the last century: poverty, class, and the cultural machinations that perpetuate these conditions.

Having seen impoverished, anonymous citizens carted in (and out) suffering from familiar and inscrutable diseases, one morning he notices that the older man across from him passed away during the night. It occurs to Orwell, as he looks with pity at the pale, broken-down body, that he's witnessing an example of death by "natural causes." And this manner of death, which so many of us literally pray for, is, he concludes, "slow, smelly, and painful." The lucky ones, Orwell notes, die at home (the truly lucky ones, he proposes, die in action, with their boots on).

Well into the twentieth century, hospitals were very much like prisons (in the literal, not metaphorical sense) only worse—particularly for the impoverished. Being there, and bearing witness, made it possible for others to see what they couldn't otherwise understand. More importantly, being there made it impossible for people to pretend these conditions didn't exist. Orwell, like Sinclair, Twain, and Dickens, did his part to parade our inhumanity and force us to confront this collective shame.

So what? Well, would it be too quaint by half (or whole) to propose that writers in general (and poets in particular, per Shelley's dictum) were indeed the unacknowledged legislators of the world? Expertise earned in the field and conferred via the discipline of expression. The best writers could acquire an old-fashioned kind of authority, the type that conferred upon an individual the honor (and obligation) of expressing truths not beholden to party lines or privilege. The type of sensibility capable of creating *1984*, for instance.

Orwell had the courage of his convictions: he enlisted, and fought in the Spanish Civil War. He took to the streets and lived as a hobo to better understand (and subsequently articulate) what life was like for those "down and out." Over time, he learned the hard way that there are no easy answers. Undaunted, he doubled down on his commitment, using these events to solidify a resolve that changing minds was more effective in the long run than bashing skulls.

iii.

You can't combat cancer with fists or poetry; you can try with chemicals and prayers, but as it is with most of our earthly affairs, it all comes down to timing and luck.

We thought we were lucky, at first. In many ways, we were, in that the diagnosis was made in time and the initial operation was successful. The cancer hadn't spread. Ten years ago, the doctor said, I would have sent you on your way. Now, knowing what we know, we'll do chemotherapy to be on the safe side.

Better safe than sorry, we all agreed.

We got lucky, we said, a year later when no cancer had come back. We were lucky, we said, all through '98 and '99, and we entered a new millennium free and clear, the cancer a thing of the past, like the Y2K bug.

A few months later we were back in the hospital. It had come back.

It was, we all agreed, time to fight. What else could we do?

When it returned a third time, in 2001, cancer once again obliged us to circle the wagons, convinced we had no options but to keep fighting, as a family. My sister asked questions, took notes, and worried. My father talked with my mother, lived with her, and ran point regarding decisions, directions, and dealing with the obligations incumbent upon anyone who has repeated the words "till death do us part." I did my own note-taking, question-asking, and behind-the-scenes improvising. Above all I envisioned the worst, hoped for the best, and lost sleep like it was my job.

During the summer of 2002, when it sometimes felt like the walls were closing in (literally, as anyone who has experienced crisis-induced anxiety can attest), I dropped pounds I didn't need to lose. I ate some good food and I drank some good drinks, but those miserable months frequently felt like one unappetizing, ill-digested meal. The worst days were when my stomach and mind simultaneously conspired against me: not enough nourishment and too much mental unrest will cause side effects even strangers notice.

Still, I knew what was at stake, and my primary responsibility, I felt, was to keep things as upbeat and optimistic as possible. This was certainly for my mother's sake, but it was also a fairly pragmatic strategy. What good, I thought, could possibly come from giving up hope, or letting my mother see the insecurity and the dread that on certain days reflected the weather: thick and humid and getting hotter as the afternoons dragged on.

But we all reserved the right to despise this disease that was decimating the woman we loved. It's not especially difficult to describe, and I suppose it's not hard to imagine the defensive feelings that boil up when you see someone close to you suffering. The fury, at times, impotently craves an outlet.

My most fervent wish, which at times became an obsession, was to swap places with my mother and take her cancer inside of me. Not in the metaphorical—or even literal—sense of preferring to struggle in another's place, although there was obviously that. It was not merely instinctual; it was personal. It was not simply a matter of wanting my mother's agony to cease, though there was clearly that. What I felt was an unappeasable compulsion to engage with this enemy. In short, I wanted to kick cancer's ass.

This was not a case of reactionary bravado or calculated displacement (though there were elements of both, obviously); this was something I would have given anything to orchestrate. There I was, in the very prime of my life, physically and, perhaps more importantly, mentally; I was as strong spiritually as I'd ever been. I was ready, and ravenous to step into the ring. It was as though I had been working my entire life to prepare for this, to assume this responsibility.

For the first time in my memory, I craved violence. I needed to step in and deal with this bullying motherfucker. I wanted to hit it, chew it, swallow it, spit it out and step on it. I wanted to laugh at it, engage it on its own terms while taking everything it had to offer, and then bury it. I saw it and I wanted it.

Of course I knew the first signs of nausea would take considerable wind out of my sails, and because I recognized it I appreciated it, and that was truly what caused me to crave some semblance of satisfaction. I am more positive of this than anything else in my entire life: if I could have done it I would have, and I would have been ecstatic.

And like everyone else who has had these exact same thoughts, I was mocked by the fact that it's impossible. Not just the fantasy of some half-assed exorcism, but the inability to do much of anything about cancer. You can't put your hands on it; you can hardly wrap your mind around it. It humbles us, eventually (inevitably) in terms of how little we actually control despite the ways we create and organize reality with clocks, calendars, words, and games. All the rituals—including faith and love—that we utilize to combat the indifference of our universe are strategies, not solutions. Cancer reminds us we are ultimately just animals in a world that promises only one outcome, and for the majority of creatures populating this planet existence is cruelly fleet and ruthlessly efficient.

The worst part? You can't make it personal. Cancer is only an organism, staying alive the only way it knows how. What can we do about that? Make it evil, invest it with the accountability for everything that can't be reconciled or explained. This is why we created the devil; it's the central reason so many of us must believe there's a benign force supervising our affairs. It explains why, with the best intentions, we determine that each misfortune is all part of a larger plan, one we can't begin to comprehend. When you go from wanting to believe to needing to believe (in something, anything) it's easier to fathom how faith can quickly lead to violence. This helps explain how—and why—knowledge was scorned or suppressed, and why men of science were burned at the stake.

It's Nature. It's natural. It's our nature.

Cancer reminds us that we're part of a natural order. Billions of organisms are attacked and invaded each day, all according to the cycle of life and death, the grim ushers in Nature's play. We are aware of it, we can use fancy jargon to explain it, we may even write poems about it. But we're pretty much powerless to do anything about it. This doesn't mean we have to accept it. Depending on how you look at the world, we fight every second of our lives just to live. Each breath we draw defies death; each thought we have outlives oblivion. Each time we give love we are defeating fear and hatred, the twin killers of compassion and connection. When we help others suffer through their final struggle we may be fighting a battle that has already been settled. At the same time, we are solving the ultimate secret of our own existence: we learn how to conquer death by anticipating it—and transcending it. This is the battle we're all born into, and it's one we are fortunate to fight as long as we're able.

Grandchildren

(1997 to 2002)

FROM LATE AUGUST 1997 through the middle of August 2002 my sister's children were our family's salvation. First the girl, six months old, all smiles, laughs (and dirty diapers) in the room where my mother recovered from that first surgery. We were all figuring out how to handle this (the situation, the operation, the prognosis, the rest of our lives) together, in real time which we found to be increasingly unreal. All the tension, distress and a sudden unfamiliarity with ourselves would have been unmanageable without a distraction. Thankfully, we had an adorable, utterly uncomplicated distraction, a gift that gave us all something to savor at a time when we may have otherwise had to fill every second with actions, words and especially thoughts.

Then came the boy, a little blonde baby born in the last week of May, easing us into the sweltering summer of 2000. A couple of weeks before the full schedule of concentrated chemotherapy commenced. How could we have made it through June and July (the heat, the hair loss, the sight of incorruptible staff pumping poison into my mother in order to make her better) without this ebullient newborn and his dedicated (and only slightly jealous)

big sister? The pictures from that period are awkward metaphors: the pale and chemical-bloated grandmother holding two beacons of immortality in her lap, their existence injecting a purpose and animation the rest of us could not begin to approximate.

Every single day between March '97 and the first week of August '02, those two kids were the things my mother loved best in the world: more than any hobbies, more than memories, more than us, more than herself. We saw this; we understood it and we accepted it. During the more difficult times we embraced it, appreciating the forces of the universe for providing a source of vitality that money and medicine do not address.

Machinery (7)
(June and July, 2002)

During the months of June and July, 2002, if the phone rang while I was getting ready for work, it meant my mother was calling. If the phone rang while I was getting ready for work, it meant my mother was calling to tell me she needed to get fluids. If the phone rang while I was getting ready for work, it meant my mother was calling to tell me she needed to get fluids and was unable to drive. If the phone rang while I was getting ready for work, it meant my mother was calling to tell me she needed to get fluids and was unable to drive, so I had to take her.

The first week of June, we'd danced together at my cousin's wedding, though she'd had a setback and almost didn't attend. From Memorial Day on, we were in somewhat of a holding pattern; we didn't know how serious the setback was. In the weeks between the last holiday of spring and the first holiday of summer, the picture gradually—and inevitably—came into focus.

Actually, it was the opposite. With the expectation (or hope) of recovery (or stabilization), tunnel vision ensues and everything on the periphery is simply a distraction. It's all a matter of scale and scope. Once you begin to lose control of the narrative, the image blurs and all the questions, conclusions, and alternatives you didn't need to consider (or didn't let yourself consider) crash in from all corners. Then, anything might happen, and while it's still a matter of scope and scale, now every possible outcome seems unacceptable.

The chemotherapy had made her sick, but it had also made her better. (Hadn't it?)

After Memorial Day, she began feeling bad again, and this time we couldn't blame it on the chemo.

Suddenly, she couldn't hold anything down, and when even plain liquids were causing side effects, it wasn't possible to kid anyone about what was going on inside her. We still didn't know, and we didn't need to know (yet), but the diarrhea and nausea became severe enough that chronic dehydration resulted.

The doctors were methodical, which was encouraging, at least initially. *She's losing electrolytes,* they said, *so we infuse those fluids into her system.* This, after all, was a miracle of modern medicine: we now had ways and means of providing what the body had trouble producing. Potassium and saline drips were prescribed to help restore the vital nutrients her body was expelling like an allergic reaction.

Solid meals and solid bowel movements became memories from another time, another life. We found ourselves in near constant crisis, spending more time shuttling her to and from treatments than we had during her regular chemo visits. That this coincided with the most intolerably hot days of summer seemed almost scripted. Nevertheless, when you see your mother shifting uncomfortably away from the blast of the car's air conditioner even though it's approaching triple digits, you are officially at the point where medicine and miracles are the only hope you have left.

Machinery (8)

(July, 2002)

I'M STANDING IN the middle of my bedroom, naked and soaking wet, reaching for the telephone. I'm shivering, not because I'm cold but because I know it's my mother on the other line and I know why she's calling.

If the phone rings when I'm getting ready for work, it means my mother is calling. And it always seems to be just as I'm stepping into the shower. I'll hear the phone ring, go to voice mail, then ring again. That second call, I've learned, means it's my mother and she's frantic to get in touch with me. It might also mean she's already attempted to get in touch with my father (who's already at work and unavailable), or my sister (who's preoccupied with her own children), and each unanswered call is amping up her anxiety.

As summer progresses, a pattern has formed: each ring now elevates my own anxiety, turning the phone into both a transmitter and conductor of distress.

It was just before July 4, because that was the weekend I started to unravel. I stood in my bedroom, having sprinted to grab the phone before it stopped ringing. (After this I would begin bringing the phone into the bathroom with me.) Less than an hour later I was with my mother, in one of the private rooms they allow you to use for the treatments.

It was around this time that I started having difficulty sitting through meetings at work. The small, windowless conference room began to feel like the stockade inside a submarine. The meeting would commence and someone would close the door (someone always closed the door) and I would immediately wish we'd left it open.

The weekend of July 4, I sat in my living room, forgetting how to breathe. I found myself pacing around the condo, breaking into a full-body sweat and eventually seeing no option but to get out, into the soul-crushing humidity. I needed to feel real air and see the sun and the trees and, if necessary, collapse onto the grass and stare up at the sky.

(*This is how it happens*, I understood. When you get sick it's seldom a real-time reaction; usually the infection is already inside and once your body begins to respond, the system succumbs. I was not unacquainted with anxiety, but I'd been fortunate never to have experienced the symptoms of a panic attack. It was during these times that I couldn't help thinking the cancer, metastasizing inside my mother, wasn't satisfied only with her. Its tentacles were long and reached out in the darkness, slipping between cars and houses, slithering over telephone lines, and crouching inside my computer. The cancer was attacking my entire family, working its way into our heads so it could take over our bodies.)

The room was cool and quiet and I held my mother's hand as she snoozed. She was ceaselessly exhausted yet seldom able to sleep, which seemed crueler than even the diarrhea and dehydration. Everyone has heard how depriving a person of uninterrupted slumber is the most effective—and sadistic—form of torture; it's insulting to the point of overkill when a sick, scared patient is not able even to rest comfortably.

The fluids worked away, silently swimming from the bag into the tube that hung above her emaciated arm. The saline drips were innocuous in almost every way: without color or scent they looked like water, the source of life. This was the same solution they dispense before and after routine surgeries, a simple process with predictable results. Lately, it wasn't a simple matter of dehydration (itself never a simple matter); her body was dangerously low on potassium, which meant a whole other series of solutions.

Once again I thought about machinery: we were back in unwelcome territory, where medications assumed a prominent role. Until now, they'd been part of a process designed to improve, however slowly or unsatisfactorily. A witches' brew of ingredients manufactured in laboratories, now replacing what her system lacked; no matter how much functionality they restored, they couldn't substitute what a body, when healthy, naturally produces. These fluids were not healing so much as supplanting, and in some subtle but insidious way they were turning her into something slightly less than human.

I was scared of the fluids and becoming more frightened by this place. I noticed the closed door (the privacy we would have killed for only last summer) and became cognizant of the nothingness surrounding me: *They clean and anesthetize this place but they can't keep it out; they're only human and they can't disguise it,* it *happens no matter what we do to prevent it and ignore it.*

My mother abruptly sat up and vomited on herself. Before I could react she retched a second time, sending a spray of fake bodily fluids onto the sheets: the color was orange and the smell was metallic. The look on her face shifted quickly from surprise to panic, and for several seconds my mind spun in a frenzy of confusion, disgust, and alarm. The smell was immediate and unprecedented: it was the scent of science and the twenty-first century, filtered through the debilitated system of a woman drowning in empty air and excruciating dread.

(Keep calm, keep it together.)

She threw up again, this time on the floor, splashing up on my feet.

(Oh my God, is she dying?)

Everything happened so quickly and I'll forgive myself if I can't recall what I said, how much I said, or if either of us said anything at all. I could have screamed or wept, or punched the wall or jumped out the window that wasn't there, but I forced myself to stay composed. I was not okay and I knew it. I was more terrified than I'd ever been in my life.

"I think you better call your father," she said.

When you've helped someone through a cycle of cancer you adapt, however begrudgingly, to the sights and sounds and smells. And it's one thing to deal with bodily secretions, no matter how malodorous or messy. Any parent or even pet owner becomes at least partially desensitized—it's an equal measure of experience, acceptance, and affection. But chemicals are another matter altogether. What erupted from inside my mother was otherworldly and unnatural, like robot blood or the sweat from a machine. It had that synthetic aroma that I recognized, but also something else, something alien yet familiar. It had a *confident* odor, as though the transmission from cold storage to overheated internal organs created some sort of grotesque entity that wanted out, that wanted to be exposed, to spread out and get inside someone else.

(It's not just the fluids; it's her cancer—that's *the cancer* coming out from inside her. It's finally here, and it's getting on you…)

(Go get the doctor.)

I found a nurse who put a call in for the doctor. I had my own call to make, so I hurried downstairs. This was near the end of the pay-phone era, and the twin machines smiled across the hall like a talk-show host: *Pick a phone, either phone; heads we win, tails you lose!* I walked over and paid a quarter to share bad news. I told my father what had happened. I told him his wife wanted him here. I told him I loved him. I told myself to hold it together, for my mother's sake. For my sake.

This is where, in the movies, the character stops and takes a long, searching gaze into his eyes reflecting back in the polished silver; maybe there's an epiphany, maybe he cries, maybe a beautiful nurse comes and rescues him. Regardless, the music swells and everyone knows something *significant* is happening. In real life, at a moment like this, you may catch a quick glance at yourself but you look away as fast as you can, afraid for what you might see looking back at you.

I needed to get back upstairs but I needed fresh air first; I needed to feel the heat caused by summer air and not my nervous system, burning itself inside out. I stepped outside of the dim lobby and the heat swirled up from the concrete and enveloped me from all sides. If this were a movie, I would question God or curse the cruelty of life or have a Hamlet moment and soliloquize about the cosmic cards we are laughingly dealt. You don't, in actuality, do any of these things. You can't; you're too busy bracing yourself as you hurtle into a black hole that swallows each thought before you can think it. You spin through space and there's no escape because it's *inner* space: we reside in our minds and once all defenses and distractions have been dissolved we speed more deeply into ourselves. When we finally fall it's not over or sideways, it's further *in*, and what's most frightening is not knowing how far we can go. We can scarcely fathom and we can hardly stand how far inside ourselves we can get…

(Get back upstairs.)

This was the worst day; this was the hardest one yet and as I got inside that elevator I knew it was going to get harder, that this might be merely the beginning of days I couldn't have imagined or possibly prepared for. I looked at my hands that were connected to arms that hung from shoulders that separated my back from my head, and I wondered what part of me had any hope of explaining, or arresting, or ameliorating any part of what lay ahead. It took the eyewitness of unreal things to fully grasp how real it had gotten, and how unreal it was likely to become. The only thing I had to fall back on was the fact that I didn't have any alternatives; I didn't have any other choice. I was scared to open the door, horrified by what I might see.

(How can I go back into that room?)

I thought, once again, about machinery and what our bodies did; what my body was doing to me. Up until now, in my own life and throughout my mother's experience, I'd had a calm understanding that I could take care of myself. I could handle whatever got thrown at me and face it without fear, because there was nothing to be afraid of. But it hadn't occurred to me that this didn't apply if confronted by the mortality of the person I loved best in the world. Presented with this, and confronted by the helplessness of having nothing to offer except kind words and assistance, I felt the fear (or was it the cancer itself?) settling inside me. The fear, like cancer, metastasizing through my family, its tentacles reaching out to ensnare each of us any way it could.

(What am I going to see when I open that door?)

As I thought these thoughts my feet, connected to my legs that took orders from my brain, continued to move forward. I kept walking and finally focused on the only thing I could: one foot in front of the other, one step closer to that room. When I got there I opened the door and went back into the room. I wasn't going to see anything I didn't expect to see, because now I expected to see things I had never seen or imagined. My eyes that were connected to my face would tell my mind what to tell my mouth and I would say the things I had to say, those things I'd never said or imagined saying. I would do this because I had to and because I had no choice. I would do it for my mother's sake and I would do it for my own sake.

Waiting Room: A Short Story

(2001)

He waits.

He looks out the window and he waits.

He doesn't look at the magazine, the one on top of the others that litter the table, the one last picked up by the last person who sat in this room.

He stands, not wanting to sit, not wanting to look down at the magazine. He looks down at the magazine, which stares up at him, defiant, disinterested, doing all that was asked of it. The magazine didn't ask to be brought into this room, it didn't ask to be read or ignored, to be picked up and put down, to be digested and then discarded.

He stands, knowing that if he thinks about the magazine he wishes he wasn't looking at, the magazine he won't read, he won't think of the things he doesn't want to think about.

He does not walk into the corridor to look into the room that his wife is not in.

He waits.

He understands—anyone who has been where he is understands—that you must prepare yourself to wait a long time. So you prepare, and you wait. And then, it's even longer than that, longer than you remember. Much longer. He remembers standing, then sitting in this room, almost the exact same spot, twice already (*third time is the charm*, he does not think) and still can't help being surprised at how long he's had to wait.

He waits.

No one talks to him (they know who he is and why he's here), and no one knows the story he could tell (it's the same story everyone who has stood where he's standing would tell).

He stands silently, shifting and sorting his awareness that eventually they will bring her to the room. When they bring her to the room he'll see her. He'll see her seeing him, then see her seeing him see her. And then she'll ask him and he'll have to tell her. He'll try not to tell her and she'll look at him and remind him that he has to tell her.

He waits.

He wishes they would hurry up (*hurry up and get it over with*, he doesn't say) and then he hopes that they'll never come so he can stand, peacefully paralyzed in this infinite instant.

Eventually, he looks at the table, and the magazine that waits for him to pick it up. He doesn't pick it up.

He sits down and doesn't think about the nothingness that surrounds him, the nothingness around him and the gnawing nothingness inside him. He doesn't notice the plants or the paintings or the cheerfully colored curtain that doesn't cover the light outside. He doesn't allow himself to contemplate the sterile silence screaming all around him, the vacant spaces, and the odd energies of dying life. Most of all, he doesn't think about *it:* how impossibly clean people in impossibly white clothes speaking impossible-to-understand languages using impossibly powerful tools and technology do everything they can but still cannot keep *it* from occurring.

He finds himself staring, again, at the magazine, the magazine that he has picked up without realizing it. He does not open the magazine that, under normal circumstances, he would not have even the slightest inclination to read. He does not open it and therefore does not, among other things, learn about which foods would improve his sex drive and help him sleep more soundly, he does not find out ways to make his partner reach new levels of ecstasy *every time*, he does not peruse his horoscope to see what the future has in store for him, he does not discover the secret to losing ten pounds in only three days, and he does not skim the interview that explains how the fragile millionaire singer lost the chance of making millions more dollars after having a nervous breakdown while filming a commercial for a soft drink she would not otherwise endorse.

He waits.

He doesn't pass the time planning opportunities that could create happiness. He doesn't deceive himself (this time) about the possibility of forgetting the present by focusing on the past. He doesn't dwell on the types of things they would enjoy doing again, the things they enjoyed, once, which they never found the time or forgot to do. Again. He doesn't think about the ways in which you discover that the things you loved, *then*, become the things that bring about inexplicable sorrow: the movies, the music, the meals, the books, the board games, the photo albums, the family.

And so: he doesn't allow himself to think about her as she is now or how she was then. Or how he is now or how he was then. How he will be.

He looks down at the magazine, again, and picks it up, again.

He understands that the second he opens the magazine they will arrive, wheeling her down the hall like the enigmatic magicians they were trained to be. If he opens the magazine, the magic act, performed (again) before an awkward audience, will begin. So he waits.

He stands up and looks out the window, at the horizon, beginning to disappear in heavy air beneath the tops of the trees. He looks down, far below, where miniature people inside miniature cars sit in miniature rows, stoically and slowly moving forward in the directions of their miniature houses and the miniature respites that may or may not await them. The sky continues to sag, ensnaring the world in its unspeaking sentry. The people, and then the cars, and then the earth all slip away, leaving only lights that sigh stoically, bearing witness to it all. He looks down at the waning waves of lights, and these lights do not look like a thousand sets of eyes, they do not make the darkness more discernible, they do not appear as poetry. They are exactly what they are: they are progress, they are pain, they are power. They are the cold logic of machines that control the lives of the men who made them.

He does not let himself think about these things. He has too many other things not to think about.

He does not turn around.

He will hear them, eventually, when they come.

Eventually they will come, and he will hear them, and then he will turn around.

Then, he will...

He looks down, again, at the magazine he will not read. He knows, again, that if he picks up the magazine they'll come.

He sits silently and stares at the magazine. He stands and looks out the window. He does not turn around.

He waits.

Interpolating a Poem

(2013)

NERVOUS AND UNNERVED this evening, alone:
Searching for solace, something not unlike prayer,
A hope that the past will not repeat itself,
Progress: a preemptive strike, this *procedure*
(They call it a procedure when
They expect nothing unexpected).
Precedence and percentages: our family has a history,
Meaning that some part of someone who has died
Might be alive and unwelcome and somewhere inside.

Remembering: immeasurable moments, IVs and all
The unpleasant things you can't force yourself to forget.
Bad days, worse days, glimpses of serenity then grief,
A flash focus of forced perspective—*this too shall pass.*
Then, inevitably, earlier times: I recall
When doctors and dentists handled us with bare hands.
Still living, then, in a past the future had not
Crept up on, a time when the truth was believable,
Because the only lies that children can tell
Get told to escape tiny troubles they've created.

(Have you ever tried to see things from cancer's point of view? What would it look like if cancers were capable of writing the stories? Let's give it a shot: *After a long, brave battle, the cancer that began in Linda Murphy's colon finally emerged victorious on August 26, 2002. Despite being assailed by chemotherapy, radiation, fear, hatred, and fervent prayers, the cancer—having been beaten back three times—remained resolute and overcame one final, furious barrage. This cancer, in killing its host, became only the latest in a long line of martyrs willing to die in order to survive. Like its host, Mrs. Murphy, it was brought into being with the end of its existence a foregone conclusion. That it struggled and persevered until the end is a credit to metastasizing cancers around the world.)*

And so I am uneasy and it's not even myself
I am thinking about: frightened all over again
For my mother, and I can do nothing for her
Now, just as I could do nothing for her, then.
A cycle: she had seen her own mother suffer
While each of them made their anxious inquiries,
Appeals entreating the darkening clouds, out of time.

Like her son, she eventually became acquainted
With the white-walled world of procedures
And all that happens—before, during, after, and beyond:
Hope and fear, faith then despair—the nagging need
To believe in men and the magic of machines.
Or the things we say when no one is speaking.

(Fourth time's the charm, I didn't say, but I knew.)

(We all did. 1997, 2000, 2001, and now 2002. Each previous time we'd avoided the verdict, dodged the bullet, lived to fight another day, embraced whatever cliché we could beg, borrow or steal.)

(This time, we knew. The surgeons would slice her open and see it. *It's in there; it's everywhere*, they would say. And then they would stitch her back together and deliver the news, all grim business. And we would bow our heads and pray for God's blessing, as we'd been instructed in those weekly services that transport ritual and inculcate compliance. Tradition, that resilient escutcheon handed down through so many generations. Which is exactly the way it happened.)

I'm so scared, she said, to anyone who was listening.
I know I was, and we hoped that God was,
The God who may have done this and a million other things
In His austere, always unaccountable way.
In the end: she feared the truth but not the reasons why
Awful things always happen to almost everyone.
Me, I envied the armor of her fear, I understood
I could not even rely on those lovely lies
About a God I can't bring myself to believe in.

We were there: a child and the man
Who brought me into this calculus.
(We are made in God's image, they say,
But it's your parents' faces you see when
You look at pictures and see the future.)

He said what needed to be said: nothing,
And I said what he said. After all,
What were we supposed to say, the truth?
The truth was this: we too were scared.

(How do you get over the loss?)

(That was the question I asked a former girlfriend who lost her father when she was a teenager. To cancer, of course. "You don't," she said. *It's just as awful as you'd imagine,* she didn't say. She didn't have to, because you can't imagine and you don't *want* to imagine. How *could* you imagine? And, oddly enough, that succinct, painfully honest answer was more comforting than it sounded. In a way, when you think about it (does everyone think about it? Are some people able to avoid thinking about it?) there's an unexpected salve in that sentiment: *You don't get over it.* Or, by not getting over it, that's how you survive it. It becomes part of you, and it is henceforth an inviolable aspect of your existence, like a chronic condition you inherit or develop along the way and manage as best you can.)

(This is important, because, as Americans, we tend to think in terms of explanations and equations: how do I *solve* this riddle? We tend to inquire: how *long* until it's okay again? I can handle the pain, I think, if I know how to endure it. Once you get your mind around the notion that the pain never goes away, it is, strangely enough, easier to incorporate into your life. You keep reading, you keep eating, you keep sleeping, you keep loving, you keep mourning, and you never stop remembering. And, above all, you keep living.)

I'm so scared, she said, and we told her
It was going to be okay, we told her
We had reason to believe and we told her
Other things when the things we'd already told her
Turned out to be untrue. We never told her
The truth, which was that we were lying.

Fear and faith are useful if you can afford either/
Or, fear is free and lingers always, longer.
After it has served its purposeless point,
Like a stain on the street, days later.
Dying is nothing to be daunted by, it's living
That takes the toll: living with death,
Living with life, being unprepared or unwilling
To be unafraid when it's finally time to die.

(*I'm so scared*, she said, more of a whisper than spoken words.)

(But more than that: she was breathless with fear. It was the dread of anticipation; the fear of expectation, and the certainty of seeing what she'd already seen.)

(My old man, balanced on the farthest edge of where he could allow himself to go, went into comfort mode, the autopilot of assurance spiked with insistence. "Relax," he said (not unsoothingly). "It will be fine.")

(It was his call, his place to have the final say. I deferred, and we left the room, the lie following us into the elevator like a solemn cloud. We drove away from the hospital separately and I have no idea what I listened to on the way home but I'm certain it helped.)

(I'm so scared, I thought, knowing we'd likely played our last hand and that we were in a rigged game the house always won. You were free to deal yourself as much hope as you could afford, but that currency can only carry you as far as the trump card the dealer is holding—the one He's always held.)

(I'm so scared, she said, and I knew she'd fall asleep. *She'll be out as soon as the lights go off,* I thought. *She's too tired and too spent to worry herself into a restless night.* Alone, in that most impersonal of places, familiar only because of its function. The only solace an awareness that, in the end, all of us go through it alone.)

(I'm so scared, she said, and I'll never forget the fear in her face or the apprehension in her voice. And I'll never forgive myself for not staying in her room to keep her company that night.)

> *I'm so scared,* I say, to anyone
> Who may be listening in the silence,
> Wondering if they can do more for me
> Than we could manage to do for her.
> There is no one left to lie to—yet
> The truth, as always, is immutable.
> And so, if you are out there, please help me
> To absolve this dread that no one can hear.

Portending
(1980, 1997)

Question: How COULD I know that dying of cancer was my mother's worst fear, the thing she dreaded most?

Answer: Because she never said so.

It was one thing she never talked about. It is, I suspect, one thing even families unaffected by this disease tend to avoid, equal parts dread and superstition. Cancer still retains its awesome sway on our collective consciousness through successive centuries, in part—or mostly—because of the impunity with which it has extinguished humans of all ages, races, and creeds. Cancer is always capable of getting our attention, so much so that it's something many of us do anything we can to avoid even thinking about.

My mother talked about her mother. I vaguely intuited then, and fully understand now, that she was also talking about herself. Not just the ways her mother's death affected her, her family, and her future, but the ways the disease might affect her, her family, and her future. She spoke about the suddenness with which her mother's illness struck, so little time to prepare, how unspeakably voracious it became once it was inside her, how quickly she had

to grapple with Death and living without the person she could never imagine Life without.

She never had to say anything directly, because every time she talked about her mother's death she was telling us exactly what frightened her the most.

So: did she come to expect the worst? I don't know. I think when she was first diagnosed, at fifty-four; she was shocked that it had come so soon. It hit her before she even had time to begin preparing for it, even if she acknowledged, on some level, that its presence was more a reunion than an inevitability.

I can't say I took any comfort in denial—however fleeting that distraction may be—because in some ways I was already preparing for this possibility before she got sick. I don't claim that this is typical, or even healthy, but it wasn't a conscious reaction. Once cancer has been introduced into your world it's impossible to eradicate it. Being old enough to understand how young my grandmother had been obliged me to grasp, if only at a subconscious level, that the disease took lives and didn't particularly care how rich, healthy, or old you happened to be.

Certainly this is true of just about any disease, but the more you learn about cancer the more you comprehend that it's just as content to claim a child as it is a senior citizen. That—aside from the number of people it kills each year and the often drawn-out, painful struggles it engenders—is what makes it such an insidious ailment. More, it's the kind of illness you can't isolate in the abstract: sure, you *could* die of a heart attack or an aneurism, but certain statistics and lifestyles make specific maladies more likely.

I didn't think my mother was destined to get cancer, so I was never resigned to the possibility. Rather, I absorbed the ways she still grappled, more than fifteen years later, with her mother's death, and the terror with which she regarded the disease. Cancer, as a concept, can become an eternally open sore, the psychic scar that could begin bleeding at the slightest touch. There were also the designated times throughout the year (her birthday, her mother's birthday, the anniversary of her mother's death) when the grieving overwhelmed all other consideration.

My father, being Irish, and a man, doesn't talk about his parents unless you ask him. And even then you need to ask specific questions (but never *too* specific). And even then there's an air of reticence, bordering on reluctance. When it comes to his past, he speaks on his own terms, and what he doesn't address sometimes says as much as what he does discuss. It is what it is, and I respect that he has his reasons for the way he's processed (or been unable to process) his past.

My mother, being Italian, and a woman, could never say enough about her mother. This was a relief in all the ways my father's stoicism is often discouraging. On the other hand, there can be too much of a good thing, especially if it ends badly and too soon. As such, the depths of her despair—the ceaseless mourning of her mother—could occasionally make my old man's reserve seem sensible.

When Words Fail

(July, 2002)

IT WILL BE OKAY.

    This is what parents are obliged to tell frightened children and what some children must one day resort to telling their parents.

    It will be okay, I said when she asked me about the nose tube. Each time they'd operated there was the inevitable nasogastric intubation, a plastic tube that is run through the nose down the throat into the stomach. The tube can be used for feeding, but in her case it was for removal of any lingering post-op detritus. Brutal but nonnegotiable: the rational mind could understand—and appreciate—that advancements like these, however barbaric they seemed to twenty-first-century eyes, did a great deal to prevent infection and hasten recovery.

    The patient with the NG tubes snaked down each nostril, however, is neither rational nor given to circumspection. Theirs is the sort of discomfort that makes forty-eight hours feel like unyielding and interminable torment.

    My mother hated those tubes to the extent that she feared them. Before they opened her up for what would turn out to be the final time, she seemed more concerned with the tubes than whatever they might discover inside her stomach. As soon as she saw the surgeon it was the first question she asked him.

"Do you think they'll need to use the tubes?" she asked me, again.

"Let's hope not," I said, a variation on the evasions I couldn't avoid.

"But the doctor said it might not be necessary."

"Well, he knows best. Let's hope he's right."

"He wouldn't say that unless it was the truth, don't you think?"

"Of course not."

"It won't be so awful if they don't have to use the tubes this time."

And so on.

It was too late: she had locked in on it and now it was all she could think about, her proclivity for obsession thrust into overdrive by this irredeemable anxiety. Once empathy eventually gave way to exasperation, I tried not to let it distract me. This was challenging not merely because I was filled with apprehension myself; I also recognized the engine that was inflaming her insecurity. I used to be that person lying in the bed, in my way. I am, after all, my mother's son.

At moments like this I had to overcome the urge to read her the riot act, for her own sake. Why let yourself get worked up, I might say. You're just setting yourself up for disappointment. Why create unnecessary stress? If they have to use that horrendous intubation we'll get past it. Try not to invest it with more power than it deserves; if you do that, you let *it* win…

And so on.

I said nothing of the sort. I knew it was too late; I knew it wouldn't do either of us any good, no matter how genuine my intentions.

It will be okay, I finally said, still holding out the slightest hope that she might be spared this nerve-shattering indignity. And when she finally fell asleep I watched her and remembered all the times she told me, patient and comforting, that it would be okay. When I didn't want her to leave my sight in a shopping mall. Or the times I got nervous before a grade-school field trip. Or when I was sick and needed to take medicine, back in the days when it actually tasted like medicine. Or when I woke up in the middle of the night, not old enough to know what a nightmare was but young enough to call out for the one person who always came. *It will be okay,* she always said, and I always believed her.

My mother always told me what I needed to hear and I gradually came to understand—and appreciate—that none of these things were a matter of life and death. Eventually I acknowledged—and accepted—that it *would* be okay, because when your mother tells you this, she knows it's the truth. She wouldn't say it unless she believed it, so I believed her.

You each get older and learn to recognize the things you can control and the things you can't. You gain perspective and experience and grasp that life goes on no matter how you wonder and worry. You might get sick and you might need reassurance but that's all part of the process, another step in your journey. You adapt and endure because it always gets better. You remind yourself: it's not a matter of life and death.

And so on.

So what can you say when, one day, it becomes a matter of life and death? What do you do when the person crying in the bed is looking to *you* for reassurance? How do you proceed when the person who always calmed you down is shuddering with fear and afraid to be alone? What else is left when actions have failed and, for the first time, even words are incapable of offering consolation? You tell your mother it will be okay. You do this because there's nothing else left to do. You say it will be okay because you know it won't and you still hope she's able to believe you.

Field Notes

(August, 2002)

Jim: Jim Boyer, oncologist, friend.
Maggie: Maggie Callanan, retired hospice nurse, friend.

Metastatic colon cancer with metastases to the peritoneum and bowel wall. Large/small intestine (abdominal area). No damage to liver, lung, or brain as far as we can tell.

Fluorouracil, Camptosar, Oxaliplatin, Herceptin, Lorazepam, Xanax.

We can't do everything we want to. But we can manage her pain better *(Jim)*.

We feel this is changing so quickly we are not sure we are able to keep up with it.

Hospice: home health, assistance with medication, communication with doctors, paperwork, help with bathing, etc. An option.

When?

Quality of life!!

Depression/anxiety: other meds that might work better/ help? Comfort issues.

Pain control. Nausea/Nutrition.

Chemo: can/should she receive? Tolerate it?

Hospice: it's time. How?

How to approach Mom with this info? Present hospice as proactive, positive measure *(Jim)*.

Question: Am I dying? Answer: Things are not looking too good today. But we are doing everything we can to manage the pain, etc. *(Maggie)*.

If she pushes the issue: deal with *this* hour, each hour. Being at home is optimal b/c of anxiety. We are making sure you are comfortable.

Be where she is. If she drifts, stay with her *(Maggie)*.

She is in transition: slowly will start focusing on herself. Backward down Maslow's pyramid, like an infant. She is in spiritual labor: rebirth *(Maggie)*.

Let her exist as peacefully as possible!

Conversation (1)

(July, 2002)

Eventually, we asked: What should we expect?

Well, we can't know for certain, they said. But at this stage you should probably begin to consider end-of-life options.

And can you point us in the right direction?

Certainly, they said. After all, we literally deal with this every day...

...

This is a conversation that never occurred, and it's one entirely too many families won't get the opportunity to have. Having not had the pleasure, I feel I'm in a safe position to suggest that, tempting though it may be, this predicament cannot necessarily be placed on doctors or even *the system*. Certainly, some surgeons and oncologists are better equipped than others (on human as well as professional levels) to conduct helpful—or at least honest—discussions regarding options, percentages, and prognoses.

...

How much time have I got? That's the big one, the most crucial, if feared question each patient eventually, inevitably asks. And if they can't—or won't—bring themselves to give voice to the concern that rips like a current through every part of their consciousness, it's up to the family to make the inquiry on their behalf. We didn't want to know, but we needed to know. We had the right to know, we felt.

Questions: Were we prepared to process it, whatever the verdict happened to be? Wouldn't the doctors tell us, finally, when it was time to confront the final stage? Isn't it our obligation to provide care and distraction, and let the professionals do what they're taught to do?

And so on.

Naturally, these questions have no definitive answers. Or worse, the answer to each one is—or can be—yes *and* no. Depending on the patient's age, or situation, or the doctor's preference, or competence, or conscience, there is probably never an adequate formula for combining truth with commiseration. Speaking only from personal experience, the worst news you can receive is not the bad news you abhor, but a deferral disguised as an alternative.

On July 20, 2002, the doctors operated on my mother for the final time. They didn't even try to remove the cancer; it was too widespread. We knew, then, that it was no longer a matter of *if* but *when*. How long have we got, we asked in direct— and especially indirect—ways, thinking (if we admitted we were thinking it) we might have a year with her, maybe only six months. It was apparent, then, and even more obvious, now, that the issue was not how much they knew but how much they didn't know. For all they knew, it *could* be a year—a miracle could occur, my mother might make medical history. And so, they declined and demurred and filled my parents' heads with words like "quality of life" and, unbelievably, chemotherapy. My mother, not knowing the truth, and my father, not yet wanting to confront it, began to embrace this potential course of action as one last bulwark against the unimaginable. *As long as we're in motion, we're still in control*: this is what I heard every time I looked at my father's face. None of us, including the doctors, could know that in a little over a month the most important question would answer itself.

It would be too easy to insist that our doctors were negligent or, at least, woefully indifferent. The reality, I suspect, is even worse than that. Obviously doctors don't want to give false hope or obliterate any remaining optimism, but the rationale for their institutional code of silence may in fact have more to do with us than them. Our country's capacity for denial is well documented; it's more likely our ever-increasing penchant for litigation that gives them pause. When the going gets tough (and the going is always tough in cancer wards), we pray doctors can perform tasks far beyond their human abilities. Even after the surgery (successful or not) has occurred, we expect these people to become priests, social workers, and saints.

Still: you want answers. Aside from comfort and serenity, those are the hardest things to come by when you're dealing with terminal cancer. No one knows anything and you get the sense that even if they did know—*especially* if they did know—they're not going to tell you.

Discussion:
Hippocrates and Hypocrites

DOCTORS TALKING ABOUT death are not unlike priests describing the horrors of hell: they speak with presumptive jurisdiction, but also an aloof conviction, almost pitying, that affirms it's not a place (death, hell) they'll ever find themselves. We can't despise them for this: without these affectations that eventually become ingrained, they couldn't conceivably perform their functions. Their comportment suggests that they've seen many of the things we pray to avoid, and have become intimate with horrors we can hardly imagine. In order to acclimate, they must first fortify themselves.

Physician, heal thyself?

It's understandable that so many of us assume doctors, who have more of everything—knowledge, money, connections—are able to take care of each other in ways their patients can't conceive. If this were indeed the case it would be comforting in a way. At least we would have irrefutable evidence that solutions do exist and we might look forward to one day employing them ourselves.

But the reality, if less polemical, is nevertheless enlightening. According to a growing field of first-hand testimonials, doctors do in fact tend to die *differently,* but not as a result of special or preferential treatment. The ultimate, paradoxical disparity lies in an intentional demurral of treatment. Less last-ditch cycles of chemotherapy or illusions of a few extra months. Which begs the complicated question: does more time with more adversity (physical if not mental) seem in any way appealing?

This phenomenon, which could simply and accurately be described as acceptance, illustrates several things. The most revealing might be that doctors, because they see so much avoidable anguish, are disinclined to die in denial when their own diagnoses stare back at them in black and white. Aware of how little can be done, and able to measure the difference between best intentions and bottom lines, some prepare accordingly. In the process, perhaps they're able to provide a measure of peace—and not the opposite—for themselves and their families.

The End

(August, 2002)

I DIDN'T NEED a doctor to tell me it was over.

On the way to no longer being, a person suffering from a terminal disease like cancer ceases to be his or herself. During this time, which is hopefully as brief as possible for all involved, family or friends (or medical staff, if they're sufficiently human) will get the message and take immediate action. The objective, you quickly ascertain, is no longer to help the person get back to being the person they were, but to help ease the resolution that Nature is not always interested in accommodating.

The five weeks beginning in late July were not unlike portions of the previous five years in miniature: good days, okay days, bad days, and awful days. But there hadn't been too many *terrible* days (most of those involved what each of us, in our own ways, experienced when we were alone, when we could finally afford to let our defenses down and enable our fears and suspicions to stalk us in the open, usually at night when the silence conspires against anyone who is hiding from something).

Eventually, and entirely too soon, based on what the doctors told us—even though they told us nothing—the worst days arrived, days worse than anything we ever could have conceived or prepared for (which might explain why the doctors don't tell you anything).

Eventually, and not entirely too late, hospice arrived. We told my mother about it, and she endorsed our decision *(What took you so long,* she didn't need to ask). The morning the nurse arrived—a gentle saint sent from heaven (because, as you may see for yourself someday, some clichés are true, and you're grateful for them)—was the worst day. My mother, shaking and distracted, an innocent bystander as pain and fear reverberated inside, each struggling to assume full possession of her decimated body.

(My sister and I looking at each other, relieved that at least we had been together—in our mother's room, in the house we grew up in—the previous afternoon, the day our mother finally succumbed, the day the pressure and the dread—at long last—had become too overwhelming for her to bear; when she told us to make the suffering go away; when she begged the God who was not in that room to help relieve her agony; when she reverted back to being the child she couldn't remember ever having been, sobbing at the impunity with which this disease assaulted her; when she resignedly looked into our eyes, no longer a mother or a wife or a woman, now just a cornered animal in a cold alley, unable to see or understand what was tormenting her, and beseeched us with a desperation I hope never to hear in another person's voice to make it stop; when she said *Please, make it stop,* and we said, earnestly and with as much honesty as we could convey, *We will.*)

Her grandchildren, the two beings she loved best of anything in the world, buzzed obliviously around that same room the following morning, the morning the nurse arrived, August 13, 2002, the moment, the exact second, she became somebody else. She frowned (she was still twitching, her system yet to respond to the new medicine she had yet to receive); her expression, first impatient, then indifferent; the way she waved her hand *(Take them out of here,* she didn't need to say). She didn't say that and she didn't necessarily think that; she was *incapable* of thinking that.

This is when I knew it was over. This is when I understood that the end had begun, because this was no longer my mother sitting—distracted and shaking—before me, this was instead a woman who had entered the last stage of a long, drawn-out, devastating dance with the illness she had loathed and feared more than anything else her entire adult life. She was no longer herself and she was no longer entirely with us; she was in a different place, that place some of us are obliged to go when our bodies then our brains are assailed, inhabited by some malignant host, and we heed a primal imperative to follow that path until we arrive at the place where we no longer need to walk or cry or breathe or believe.

Fairy Tales and Feeding Tubes

(August, 2002)

BETWEEN HER FINAL surgery and the arrival of hospice was our experiment with the feeding tube. This apparatus, which connected to the port installed for previous chemo treatments, was sufficiently impractical and unsavory that it seemed a small, if conflicted victory when we agreed to discard it.

"So just call us if you have any questions or trouble using the tube," the nurse at the hospital explained.

My mother frowned. "But...can I not *eat* anymore?"

"Oh, well, you can," the nurse said with a smile, employing the loud and cheerful voice reserved for the very young, the very old, and the terminally ill. "You can just chew the food and then spit it out."

The boxes of liquid nourishment they sent us home with looked like tins of cat food stacked one atop the other. It was, literally, dehumanizing: more chemicals and contraptions to facilitate what her body could no longer manage on its own. But, we knew, some people can make peace with this sort of situation and exist indefinitely, assuming their systems hold up. My father thought (or hoped) this solution would boost her strength, buy some time. For my part, I suspected it was the first clear signal that things were headed, irretrievably, in the wrong direction.

People say they'll try anything, do whatever they can to extend life—and they mean it. But when you're obliged to receive sustenance in a manner that more closely resembles a car getting gasoline, it's surprisingly easy to draw lines in the sand.

"I didn't want to disappoint him," my mother sobbed, overcome with exhaustion and relief, the day we placed the tube alongside the pile of unused tins. She was referring to my father, the husband and scientist who, to this point, was still processing—and proceeding—as though these were problems that could be solved. Time for an appointment? Drive to the facility. Questions and concerns? Speak to a doctor. Vomit or feces on the bathroom floor? Clean it up. Helplessness and the smothering waves of hopelessness? That's what prayers are for.

And so, here's where we found ourselves.

The good news: no more feeding tube.

The bad news: you are going to die.

. . .

Here's the thing about acceptance: we all had time to prepare and adapt. My mother, finally, after opening every door and stumbling down every last alley, had no other choice but to accept. Sometimes the choice makes itself when there's nothing left but a choice that will make itself. She finally accepted where we were and what was coming.

Even with the best of intentions we waited too long to bring in hospice. We didn't understand that at a certain point even a single day is too long. In shockingly short order, her body had deteriorated to the point of its final betrayal: she could no longer digest food.

"Your body can no longer digest food," my father said.

It was five days after hospice arrived, three days after my aunts arrived, a million years since her first surgery; another century, another lifetime.

My father, my sister, and I stood around the bed, finally confronting the moment that, after all denials, medical interventions, and best wishes otherwise have failed, arrives at last. The only comfort is that at least it's not a doctor telling her; at least she's in her own home.

"Do you understand what this means? Do you understand what I'm saying to you?"

"But what about Gandhi?" she asked.

Nobody knew what to say to that.

Gandhi lived for weeks without eating...

My father smiled, but my sister and I did not. Neither did she. To this day, opinions vary as to whether this was my mother's sense of humor shining through—her attempt to convey acquiescence with resolve and élan. I was not—and am not—able to believe this interpretation, and I very much wish I could, because it would make it so much easier to recall the look on her face.

I didn't see a dying woman bravely acknowledging that last inevitable. I saw a frightened woman resisting the pitiless assessment most cancer patients must withstand. She seemed unbearably innocent and vulnerable, like a child trying anything to prolong bedtime. *Just one more story*, she was saying. One more chance; one last reprieve.

(Remember Rip Van Winkle? Maybe I could just go to sleep and when I wake up, a month or a year from now, the cancer will have forgotten all about me...)

Little pig, little pig, let me come in.
No, no, not by the hair on my chinny chin chin.
Then I'll huff, and I'll puff, and I'll blow your house in!

(No! What about Scheherazade and the thousand and one nights? How about if we just tell stories and keep talking so we can outlast Nature?)

(You can't put the genie back into the lamp!)

(No! What about Christ in the desert? Forty days and nights...)

The spirit is willing but the body is weak...
Father, if You are willing, take this cup from me...

We knew what was coming and she knew what was coming, but the last days seemed more like the concluding act of an extended production. As the credits rolled you could appreciate, in hindsight, all the plot twists, clues, and assorted characters: the heroic nurses and the imperious surgeons; the absent friends who failed and the family members who pulled through; the quietly restorative acts of strangers and the redemptive solace of favorite artists. And, above all, the unwelcome reminder that happy endings occur only in fairy tales.

War and Peace

(August, 2002)

THE END OF my mother's life was as peaceful as possible, but only because we took deliberate measures to ensure that it was as peaceful as we could possibly make it. Being in the relative—and comparable—comfort of her own home was a crucial start for any sort of positive ending. Having a supportive hospice nurse dropping by every other day guaranteed that she would not be distracted by noise, bureaucracy, and other patients.

I didn't know until I had to know, so I wonder how many people know (and I hope they don't know if they never need to know) how *end-of-life pain management* actually works. In addition to the professionalism and experience hospice brings to any situation, there are the drugs (morphine, to be precise) administered to alleviate pain. Here's the catch: the more pain the patient feels, more drugs and higher doses are required.

We quickly understood the stakes: the more morphine we used, the less lucid my mother would be. The more aggressively we managed her discomfort, the less coherent—and present—she would become. This, for a short period of time that lasted entirely too long, was territory my father felt uneasy entering.

"You could be getting more medication than we're giving you," my sister explained.

Our mother looked confused.

"We could give you more…" my sister started.

Our mother nodded, then closed her eyes.

"But Dad is concerned…well, he wants you to be as lucid as possible…"

Our mother opened her eyes, then shook her head. "For what?" she said.

. . .

A few words about my father. His compulsion to be in control is what enables him to function, it's what made him successful, it's what makes him reliable, and it is, on occasion, what makes him intolerable. But this is how certain men, particularly men of his generation—especially Irish Catholic men from Boston—operate. There simply is no concession for half-measures: if you betray a single soft spot, this weakness exposes a fault line that cracks open and swallows your entire being.

And so, we found ourselves in an untenable place where morphine, which represented compassion, common-sense, and, ironically, control, was clashing against religion, which represented fear, impotence, and, worst of all, negligence. My old man, in short, was still taking orders from a force that my sister and I no longer respected. It was a force we'd found conspicuously absent, a week before, when my mother pleaded, first with God, then with us, to do something, to try anything in our power to take away her pain. *That* was the person—and the imperative—I intended to comply with.

Fights, fortunately, had been infrequent during the last five years. Few things can rally (or, I reckon, splinter) a family faster than terminal illness. I could hardly recall the last time I'd even exchanged unpleasant words with my father; mostly I'd said "Let me know what you need" and "I love you." This is what we all said to each other, implicitly, in almost every conversation over the course of five years.

And here I found myself, as my mother got busy with the business of losing the biggest battle of her life, realizing I had to square off with a man who was finally confronting the one scenario he couldn't control.

...

A few words about this fight. It was a minor miracle that it hadn't already happened. It could have happened, and under less extreme circumstances *would* have happened, ten days before. That was the morning my mother sat in her kitchen, agitated and unable to stop shaking, with what little indignity remained boiling to the surface. She had gone from tolerating, then loathing, to finally dreading this alien presence that kept kicking her when she was down. Alongside the feelings of betrayal about a system that had already checked out on her, amongst the confusion and exasperation that made a mockery of time and sense, underneath the ticking of the bomb her body had become, above all these competing concerns was the onset of a sustained and suddenly irrepressible sense of foreboding.

My sister and I looked at each other, nervous and unsettled: this was new territory, and we had no clue how to negotiate it. Neither did our father, and it was apparent, in this precise moment as the four of us sat around the kitchen table—a family routine frozen in time—that he wasn't following this new narrative, our personal *War and Peace* that came without CliffsNotes. He grabbed his keys and my sister glared at him: *Where are you going?*

Where do you think, he said.

And we knew: he was going to church. It was Sunday morning so he was doing what he'd done every Sunday morning, without a single exception, throughout his life. And I knew: his wife needs him but he needs his routine. He needed it more desperately than any of us could even fathom. And in that moment I despised him for it.

"Can't you just stay?"

This was my mother. She looked at him, incredulously, more angry than sad. "Can't you just sit here and hold my hand?" To which this good man—this loyal husband who had thus far done everything he could, who had walked with her every step of the way from day one, who could not fairly be described as anything but fully committed—smiled (it might have been imperceptive, it may have been ambivalent, it could have been complacent, but it was not in any way *guilty)* and walked out to his car. I wanted to follow him into the garage, hold him down and force feed him pages from the bible. And the one thing that stopped me was the realization (clear in that instant) that he was not okay. His flight was not (merely) answering the call of ritual and obligation. He wasn't ready, yet. He was, in fact, very aware of what was happening. He was scared and he was running for his life.

...

Fuck that, I said, finally ready to fight, the day he protested the boosted dose of morphine. Pray all the accountability onto me, I don't care. We can't afford to defer to a bunch of magical thinking right now. You may be worried about going against God's will, or you may have your own preferences, but we're more worried about our mother. We will not allow her to be afraid and in pain.

I wanted to say this, and my father needed to hear it. But the circumstances were too severe for misplaced passions. Instead, I did the only thing I could to make my case in a way that authority (his or His) or arguments could not lightly counter: I wept. I held my sister's hand and we told him we couldn't abide seeing the woman upstairs suffer. Still, it was his call, so we implored him to authorize the level of medication our hospice nurse saw fit to provide. That's what she's here for, we cried.

It wasn't easy for our father; he had been there for everything. Even the things he hadn't been there for, because nothing we saw when he wasn't around was anything he hadn't already seen. But he hadn't been there the week before, when my mother couldn't keep still in her bed, the cancer slithering around her insides like an eel. He hadn't heard her say what she said or seen us promise what we promised. And so it was our obligation to convince him to take that last step and join us on the other side, where our mother was already waiting.

Deus ex Machina

(August, 2002)

WAS THAT AS bad for you as it was for me?

That's the question I didn't ask when Father _____ left our house. On to his next appointment, all in a day's work.

Extreme unction: the old-fashioned term for that quaint custom. It serves its purpose even now, I suppose, but I couldn't help thinking on this particular occasion it's more often a ritual designed for everyone except the person lying on his or her death bed.

Speaking only for my mother, she was too busy dying to want, much less appreciate, the solemn incantations and grim officiating on offer. It didn't help matters that our local church's current pastor had a personality that made even the surgeons we'd dealt with seem convivial. It wasn't his fault; he was an older man from an older school: the twenty-first century didn't suit him, just like it wouldn't suit over-the-hill academics and the stratified folks still clinging to every *ism* they could get their claws on. The world keeps spinning and younger, more insolent models keep popping up to replace you. Some learn how to take this in stride; others resist and end up like insects flying against traffic. And some just disengage and surf that sluggish wave into the safe haven of senility. Father _____ was of the latter ilk; it wasn't that he was going through the motions so much as the motions were going through him.

And who could place blame at the exhausted feet of a man ten years past retirement age? Not I. Can you imagine earning your living re-reading the same book (no matter how much you enjoyed it the first thousand times; even if you believed that as soon as the words left your humble lips they ascended straight to God's impossible ears) and knowing, every day, how this particular story ended? Worse, telling a tale with a conclusion that already occurred, since everything we do—if you follow this narrative—has already been plotted out in that great workshop in the sky. And all this role required was that you promise to anyone willing to listen the same salvation you could never be sure of; no matter how certain you were, no matter how achingly every aspect of your existence relied on this deus ex machina.

Father _____ had quite apparently made peace with his place in the world (or worse, resigned himself to it) long enough ago that by now every rote gesture was divorced from anything approaching passion. But was passion, in his case, even a prerequisite? He was, at this point, incapable of being surprised by anything: in certain vocations this might signify the highest possible level of proficiency.

In any event, I couldn't know—and didn't particularly care—if his visit was doing anything for him (that was between him and the surprise ending awaiting him once he got a taste of his own unction). I knew it was doing something for my old man, so I contented myself with the diminishing returns of dubious blessings. Pops was receiving the same dispensation he attained at each Sunday service: a box checked off, a chore completed, an obligation fulfilled. It was, at best, a somber sort of solace, but I certainly wished, for his sake, it was bestowing some measure of spiritual respite.

"Does she want to receive communion," the holy man said, more a statement than a question as he reached for his stash, a to-go Eucharist in what looked like a Tupperware container. At that moment he more than a little resembled a parent ready to placate an unruly child with a treat, and I realized (reflecting on this later) that my observation signaled the tipping point of an extended but ultimately unsatisfactory experiment with the Catholic faith. The priest's indifference (even worse than the indignation he may have managed in his younger years) when my father broke the news that his wife was not able (none of us could say she was not willing, but we all had our opinions) to partake didn't rankle me as it might have in my younger years. If this had gone down a decade earlier, I wouldn't have yet seen enough of the world—and the ways it wears on all of us—to appreciate how even the noblest occupations are, at the end of the day, a way to put bread on the table, even if that bread is supposed to signify the body of Christ.

It wasn't anger I felt, just relief that when finally confronted by the thing I feared most in the world, I was neither willing nor able to clutch at the redemption he stuck back in his coat pocket. I couldn't feel disappointed and I dared not feel pity; what, after all, did I know about all he'd seen and the things he felt? I hoped then, and hope even harder now—though I'm not quite willing or able to pray—that he was still alive somewhere inside, or had been at one point. I hoped, although his extremities were growing cold, that an ember of faith and hope blazed warmly somewhere inside the recesses of his worn-out heart.

Discursion: Faith (4)

Blessed are they who mourn, for they shall be comforted.
Blessed are they who hunger for thirst and righteousness, for
they shall be satisfied.
Blessed are the merciful, for they shall obtain mercy.

My mother had a different type of faith.

"Being a Christian is a fine thing," she did not say. "But *acting* like one is even better." She might have said that if she ever said things like this. She didn't need to: she simply ensured I would make this connection on my own, not while I was daydreaming during a Sunday service.

To my mother's way of thinking, church was perfectly acceptable in theory, and more than occasionally in practice. Her way of relating to the world, and the actual people who populated it, emphasized the spiritual over the Holy Spirit. Actions spoke louder than psalms, but prayers had their own special power and she believed something could hear her when she spoke without speaking.

She was brought up, like my father, by parents who endorsed the idea that their pope was God's human vessel and the concept of speaking infallibly was not farcical. As such, she had religion beaten into her, like most Catholic immigrants did. God was at once the author of existence yet above the often grim conditions he chaperoned. Boys, who get the bruises, got off easily; girls received the sort of scars that never heal because they occur on the inside.

She married a man who regarded religion less as an institution than an obligation: his perspective—like all successfully inculcated Catholics—could seem more obsessive than spiritual. He knew his scriptures, absorbed the Ecumenism, and most importantly never missed a Sunday mass. Ever. She did not, and could not, challenge the manner in which her children were brought into the church. In a way, this was easier; if mass was akin to death and taxes—if slightly more tolerable than either—it became another immutable part of the routine. In other words, she accepted that for many Catholics, church was like work: you needed to show up and put in the time if you hoped to get compensated.

She was a believer. She believed (wanted to believe? needed to believe?) that she would see her mother again, that all of us could one day hold hands in Heaven. Not literally, of course, but once one accepts that our affairs are entirely in God's figurative hands, metaphors are an adequate if obligatory indulgence.

The impulse that feeds faith is powerful, and when life seems cruel or senseless the impulse can become a compulsion. Practically everything we witness during our time in this world obliges us to seek solace in some sort of plan, a deference to that prime mover who, unmoved, aligns the stars that dictate our inscrutable destinies. This recompense, the relieving belief in a higher authority arbitrating our affairs, ameliorates some of the mendacity, injustice, and unfulfilled wishes that comprise the majority of our experience while we live.

It's difficult to say whether Christianity shaped my mother's sensibility or appealed to her intrinsic sense of fairness. The New Testament resonated, which is consistent with people who are interested in emulating and not merely obeying. Indeed, the types of so-called Christians who seek inspiration in the Old Testament are typically proselytizers or repressed opportunists looking to find ecclesiastical back-up for their very human prejudices and desires.

> *Whatsoever you do to the least of my people, that you do unto me.*

Jesus, ideal as an inspiration if not the revealed truth. How can you not get behind this example, this *idea* that is larger than faith? *God is Love; Without Love I Am Nothing.* This doesn't leave much room for interpretation, no matter how consistently the dominant themes of this man's teachings are neglected or appropriated for our unevolved times. This is where the scripture and the rule-following (and the rule-creating) men in charge of laws and wars miss the heart within the words they claim to worship.

> *For I was hungry and you gave me food, I was thirsty and you gave me drink, I was a stranger and you welcomed me...*

This is the kind of decorum you can spend many Sundays (some folks spend their entire lives) trying to understand in a church. It sounds good when you hear it, and it may even be inspiring if the man on the altar conveys it with sufficient humility. But like so many aspects of organized religion, it's when the rhetoric matches reality in the streets that it affects the soul.

A Time for Ghosts (2)

(2002)

SHE SITS ALONE by the window.

She hears the old clock, spinning above the fireplace as it always has, serving its simple purpose. Above her, a picture, a moment secure in time. In her mind, in her memory. The man, a lifetime of work and fatherhood ahead of him. And who is that woman smiling back at her? What thoughts were in that hopeful bride's head? The same thoughts that are most likely behind every face that knows the assurance of love. What would she tell her younger self now, if she could? Everything? And to what avail? She would not have believed it; this is the redemption of youth. Who should think about anything else when all a young woman knows is the security of a healthy heart, the shuttle that spins life and expedites the enduring labors of love? She would say nothing. She has no regrets; she has done the best she could.

She closes her eyes and hears her mother: *He's beautiful.* Yes, a girl and then a boy. Perfection, completion. Her prayers answered both times. She sees her daughter, married and once more a mother (a girl and then a boy; all of their prayers answered, again). She sees herself, a grandmother, but still a mother. A woman, a wife.

She considers her son and focuses her energies on his evolving design, the visions he shares with her, the way he sees himself, the way he hopes he can be. She prays it will happen, she wishes it might happen for him as well. He hasn't found a soul mate yet but she no longer worries about him; he has found himself. His writing keeps him company and it helps keep her alive; their discussions, the things they love and share, the things he still wants to learn. Hopefully he will live that life and find ways to record what he sees.

She envisions the future and sees her husband, alone or at least without her. He would have to learn new routines, she knows. He would also have the time to recall some of the things work and married life have prevented him from pursuing. She hopes he will feel contentment if he reconnects with things that matter only to him. Mostly she prays for him to find peace, without her and for himself. She prays and worries for him, and then for the people she knows and the people she has never met. And, eventually, for herself.

It is cold. The air outside her window is sharp, somber. Winter, but soon enough it will be spring.

It is the time of day when, for a moment, the world becomes silent while the evening prepares for its seraphic sentinel. It is a time for reflection. A time for ghosts. This is what she has now, and what she thinks about—the sufficiency of her thoughts and especially her deeds. She thinks about her life; who she is and what is to come.

Gifts and Messages

(August, 2002)

YOU WAKE UP and look at her, still there. You watch her sleep. Her mouth is moving: she is talking to people. She wakes up and tries to look at the watch she is not wearing. She sees you and asks what time it is. You tell her and she asks if you are watching her sleep.

Is that okay?

Yes.

. . .

How soft and calm and beautiful her voice was. How gentle and warm she felt. How you lay beside her and placed your head on her arm and held her hand and she rubbed your face softly with her other hand.

How she felt the tears on her arm and saw that you were silently shaking.

You are emotional today.

I was just thinking about how much I love you.

That's nice.

Everything that is good about me is because of you.

You gave me a lot to work with.

Everything's going to be okay.

That's good.

. . .

Another gift: Sunday afternoon as she peacefully napped by her-self. You went in and sat next to her. She woke up and reached for you.

Are you tired of sitting around?

No, I'm fine. I'm great, everything is okay.

Hold me tight.

She took your hand and put her other arm around your head. You lay without talking for a couple of hours. After a while you realized you were ready, beginning to sense (even hope?) that she might pass right there—quietly, content. But her breathing was still heavy and deep and her grip on your hand surprisingly strong. So you began to think: she might have some fight after all, plenty of life left inside.

And as you watched her you kept thinking: she is so tranquil, so silent, so beautiful.

. . .

More gifts. Time, not just all this time, but time itself. As fast as everything went last week (and this year, these past five years), it's been the opposite this week: everything has slowed down and you've all withdrawn from the world to exist (as long as neces-sary; as long as possible) inside this house, inside your love. She's at peace and not in pain, not entirely here and not entirely there; she's in transition and you're all following her lead. This transi-tion has been calm and soothingly slow. Time itself is somehow outside of you and you're outside yourselves, on the inside.

...

Lying there again, in the near darkness, with no distractions (no words, sounds, TV, music, people) and just experiencing the ultimate kind of closeness. Putting your head on her shoulder and her putting her fingers in your open mouth as you breathe, just letting her find that place and rest them there, covering that hand with kisses, the softest reassurance you could offer. Having felt the most inexpressible anguish these last weeks this is the most redemptory sort of satisfaction; something approximating peace and almost, unbelievably, joy.

...

Try to remember. Never forget this: how calm she is as she sleeps, how oddly *alive* she seems, even as she is very obviously slipping slowly away. Asleep but speaking (to whom?), talking to people not in the room but clearly (hopefully) in her mind and especially in her heart.

...

Don't worry about anything, everything's going to be okay.
Okay.
Don't worry about Pop, I'll take care of him.
How...
I'm never going to leave him. I'm going to take care of him.
Take care of him.

...

In the end you try to do for them what they did for you.

You watch them, filled with concern and fear, hoping that love and care can be enough. You sit there, quiet, trying to radiate what you don't feel inside—trying to resist all the doubt and grief, the concern and fear. Please, you ask, just let her be peaceful; after all this, allow her to finally find peace. Looking right at her, all over her, you do what you can to provide some semblance of peace. By meditating, thinking, focusing (the type of concentration that eventually brings clarity), and trying to will everything to be okay (*Everything's going to be okay:* this is the one promise you've repeated these last two weeks; a message and a mantra). Three hours. Unloading an internal barrage of comforting, healing thoughts and images, offering up everything that's ever inspired you: snippets of songs ("While My Lady Sleeps" by Coltrane and "Blue Nile" by his wife Alice, and dozens of others), even fragments of poetry and prose (Ivan Illich: *Death is over!*; Emily Dickinson: *Because I could not stop for death, He kindly stopped for me;* Keats: *When I have fears that I may cease to be;* Shelley: *The lone and level sands stretch far away*) and finally thinking, then silently humming the first nursery rhyme you can recall hearing: *Go to sleep, go to sleep, go to sleep.* Then imagining it as a song, then *hearing* it (composing it?) as a jazz improvisation, with or without words, hearing a trumpet state the theme, then a sax, then the piano, then cymbals cascading in with a warm wash, until it takes off, soaring beyond music, beyond consciousness and somewhere else altogether...

Where were you?

Somewhere else. Out of body but in your mind? Shivering with purpose, glistening with energy and faith—faith in the energy inside, getting back to being inside this house, this situation, inside of yourself. Beginning to appreciate that you can't (shouldn't?) try to understand everything, especially the things you seek to understand most of all. Just fear and concern becoming concentration, concentrated energy ending up on the other side as love.

Reversal

(August, 2002)

THE IDEA IS that, in theory, as your parents age you assume some degree of responsibility for them and, to some degree, you take care of them when they can no longer take care of themselves. This cycle begins, in theory, the second you're born—setting a natural process of physics in place—and is accelerated by terminal illness.

As this scenario unfolds, you forget almost entirely about yourself and steadily put all your energy, hope, and attention toward someone else. It's a reversal of the process every parent initiates when they hold their baby for the first time: *This* is my life now; everything I do must revolve around this child's safety. The first and foremost obligation of any mother or father is to make sure their baby stays alive.

There is, in theory, an intermediate stage, which occurs when you watch one or both of your parents' parents pass away. After my father's mother died, leaving him an orphan (in theory) at fifty-one, one of my first thoughts was: I have to have children now; I've got to keep the line going and preserve the family name. I was twenty-one. Arguably that was Society, under cover of Cliché, thinking those thoughts and putting that familial imperative at the forefront of my mind. But there's undeniably something instinctive about this circling of the genetic wagons: we see it in virtually every species—that innate compulsion to create and protect.

...

With end-of-life caretaking there are no half-measures: once the inevitable becomes apparent, there's nothing but total commitment. I had one unambiguous objective, which was making sure—after having already done everything I could to prolong life and obstruct suffering—that death was peaceful. What does this, in actual practice, mean? It means ensuring that the person dying is not alone. And what does *that* mean, exactly? Not in a hospital. And never alone, literally. From Monday, August 12 until Monday, August 26, my mother was not by herself for a single second. This became our collective mission, and an undeclared obsession: *this* was the least we could do.

My mother's two oldest sisters—the two aunts I had always been closest with—were present for what turned out to be the final eleven days, and we all took turns doing the things that needed to get done: making food, washing dishes, doing laundry, administering medication, changing clothes, talking, listening, crying, laughing, worrying, remembering, reminding, and reinforcing. My father, sister, two aunts, brother-in-law (when he wasn't at work or tending to two young children), and I split the days into segments, guaranteeing that someone was awake and alert, stationed at or near my mother's bedside at all times.

For the first week this was almost entirely for my mother's sake. She was still coherent, occasionally uncomfortable, and experiencing brief but acute flashes of distress. By the second week we were acting in interests that were more communal: being present, taking the opportunity to experience time slowing down and languidly turning away from the outside world. Except for welcoming the visits of the hospice nurse, we had a decreasing level of care or even awareness that on the other side of our air-conditioned fortress the late August heat was keeping its own kind of time—the kind measured in minutes and on calendars.

The primary apprehension, also unspoken, was not being there: *What if I'm not here when it happens?* Being stationed in the house I grew up in, it seemed that much more inconceivable to imagine going anywhere else, or falling asleep, or eating, or showering, et cetera. We were on high alert. The stakes were conspicuous and we understood our responsibility—to her and to each other.

Being able to say a long, slow goodbye turned out to be the best gift we could ever have given, or received. My aunts and I have often recalled the shared impression that those were the two most exhausting, emotional, unexpectedly exhilarating weeks of our lives. Helping someone die is a luxury, and the hardest job you will ever love.

. . .

You learn how to take care of someone when you're obliged to take care of someone. Anyone who has had a child, or even a puppy, understands how this elemental injunction follows its own perfunctory mechanism. It's a combination of the most basic principles of cause and effect and a cognition of accountability. It's an experience that alters perception. Even as the actuality of your world is made inexorably smaller, the ways you view the world inside and around you—the connections with others and the parts of yourself you scarcely knew—are sharpened and expanded.

...

It was a blessing, possibly a miracle.

We could all see her steadily slipping away, more there than here, her body (and mind?) already in places we couldn't access or imagine. It was good; it felt right; we had all said the things we needed to say, and she had heard every word. We each had our time (we wanted more but we also grasped, even then, how fortunate we had been to get this extended, uncomplicated opportunity), and we were, at this point, more witnesses to than participants in her very personal, peaceful retreat.

Would she die on her birthday? It was plausible, even perfect in its peculiar way, but not anything any of us actively wished for (at a certain point you don't expect or even hope, you simply wait). Her experience was unfolding at its own pace, so be aware (we thought), be engaged, be *prepared*.

"I feel like there's dust on here," she said, running her hands delicately along the sheets.

"No, it's clean, it's okay."

"Oh. It feels dusty."

"No, it's okay. You're clean, you're beautiful."

"That's good…"

This was one of the last semi-lucid conversations I made it a point to record (another entry in another journal, another endeavor to document the story of my life). I was ready. I hoped she was ready. I was able, for the most part, not to read too much into her words, or find metaphors in the morphine. It's clean, all right, I thought: everything ordered and its appropriate place. Of course she's telling me something with this, whatever it might be. More importantly, I was able to hear it, and then tell *her* something.

She slept. She knew it was August 23, her birthday. We knew too, and made sure she remembered. She was still there; still with us. I'd like a coffee frappe, she said, and it was not medication or the specter of death speaking, this was a woman who knew who and where she was, recalling the treat she had loved most since childhood, when she could get frappes in the only place they make them properly: Boston. My father, who knew a thing or two about Boston and authentic frappes, sprang into action. He went to the store and purchased the necessary ingredients, and we did our best to approximate the real thing. My sister and my aunts did what my mother had always done for everyone else: they baked a cake and around 8 p.m. we brought in the goods, singing Happy Birthday.

A miracle or something more: she sat up, smiling, and proceeded to enjoy what all of us knew would be her last celebration. She sipped the frappe and ate a little bit, just enough cake, slowly, contentedly. She was there and she was with us. *We did right by her,* I wrote. Just like she always did for everyone else, all her life.

. . .

After that, we were ready. She was ready as well, we hoped. What more could we ask for? Incredibly, we got more. After two days of serenity, where even when we helped her to the bathroom she hardly opened her eyes, we supposed we had enjoyed our last opportunity to communicate with her. We were wrong. Almost exactly forty-eight hours after we serenaded her with birthday wishes, my father leaned in to kiss her goodnight. Immediately, she became animated and hugged him, kissing him and saying things (hurriedly, excitedly, lovingly) that we could not hear across the room. He heard them, and said some things of his own, and we sat back, awed and grateful for another remarkable moment. For a second or two I may even have caught myself wondering if she was, in fact, ready—or willing—to ease into that final night's sleep. How can she be so *present* and purposeful, I asked myself. How can it be possible that she's closer to death than life?

I was thinking these things as I leaned in close for my own goodnight kiss. I felt her arms around me, her lips on my check, and for a half hour that felt like forever we held one another. I was, once more, able to tell her all the things I wanted to say; all the things she needed to hear.

. . .

It all seemed too good to be true, and then it got better. But first, it got much worse. After we all had our extended (final?) farewells, my mother sank back into semi-consciousness and we were certain that she would pass quietly during the night.

As I had done most evenings during the last two weeks, I slept beside her, far enough on the other side of the bed to allow her all the space she needed, and not interfere with whatever she might be doing or wherever she was in the process of going. As the night passed she became increasingly restless, jerking her body with a force I would have thought unmanageable. She was obviously agitated, and her movements made it more difficult for her to draw breath. By early morning she had woken me up again, her voiceless sounds suggesting she was in an altogether different place than she had been for the last several days. But where, and why? I moved in and stared down for several seconds, trying to see if she was attempting to express something.

This continued for hours, and our collective anxiety escalated as we struggled, without success, to determine what was causing her restlessness or what we could do to assuage it. How can this be happening, I thought, feeling sorry for her and, by extension, the rest of us. It seemed unfair to the point of cruelty, being forced to watch this late development we could neither control nor comprehend.

Finally, my father discovered the problem. We were so preoccupied with her spiritual state it hadn't occurred to any of us that she hadn't been out of her bed for at least a full day. My mother's body, though barely responsive to outside stimuli, still had its most basic functions to perform. She had wet herself, soaking her underpants, nightgown, and the sheets. All at once, the cause of the disquiet she could not convey was apparent, and for us, appalling.

Action saved us from deliberation, and we moved quickly to improve the situation. It required all five of us to gently lift and hold her in place while we wiped and powdered her, after removing and changing the sheets. The aerial view in the movie of my mind tracks the people who knew her best and loved her most working in concert; deliberate but calm, transferring the air of anger and culpability that had almost sabotaged our best intentions. It was the entirety of the last five years condensed into one gesture, a collective act that required tenderness and tenacity, accessing previously untested stores of devotion and faith. In the space of several minutes we confronted a situation that rekindled our worst fears and ended up reinforcing our best aspirations, resulting, finally, in a unique, oddly familiar solace, as though we'd been waiting to receive it our entire lives.

Once we had her back in place she settled into a deep, secure sleep she never woke up from. Finally, irrefutably at peace, she remained so for the rest of the afternoon. We could feel it as the sun set behind us and the house grew cooler and darker. We kept up our vigil while her breathing slowed to the point where, eventually, we could almost perceive her heart drawing the blood back into itself.

Nothingness
(2002)

i.

When I have fears that I may cease to be
Before my pen has glean'd my teeming brain,
Before high piled books, in charact'ry,
Hold like rich garners the full-ripen'd grain...
When I behold, upon the night's starr'd face,
Huge cloudy symbols of a high romance,
And think that I may never live to trace
Their shadows, with the magic hand of chance...

THIS PARTICULAR WORK resonates with each successive generation because it grapples with the most profound fear any of us will ever experience: the acknowledgment that one day we will perish, not knowing what actually awaits us once we're gone. That John Keats, easily one of the incontestable geniuses of any era, had several decades—at least—of his life stolen by a vulgar disease tends to augment the import of his solemn meditation. There is nothing anyone can say that could possibly begin to explain or rationalize this travesty of karmic justice, this affront to life.

It's enigmas like these that make certain people hope against hope that there's a bigger purpose and plan, a way to measure or quantify this madness. But in the final, human analysis, whatever we lost can never subdue all that we received.

Does it make a difference if he's no longer around, if he never knew his words would be read, studied, and savored centuries after he drew his last breath? Was he hoping he might witness that as he wrote the words; are we hoping we might see it when we read them? The questions are unanswerable, and the only thing we can be certain about is that he did live, he did write, and we do read. That's not nearly enough in terms of consolation for his death, and our loss, but it helps. As always, with art, it helps that we will always have the gifts the artist left behind. It's never enough; it's more than enough.

It's enough to make us consider asking more unanswerable—and unsatisfying—questions, like: "What kind of God would take a poet like Keats from us?"

Asking questions like that can lead us to answers that are at once the easiest and most difficult to understand or accept: "The same one who gave him to us?"

This, of course, isn't enough. It's never enough.

But somehow, it will have to do.

ii.

> *And when I feel, fair creature of an hour!*
> *That I shall never look upon thee more,*
> *Never have relish in the faery power*
> *Of unreflecting love!—then on the shore*
> *Of the wide world I stand alone, and think*
> *Till Love and Fame to nothingness do sink.*

He thought about his life.

(There is no sight so surreal as your mother being picked up, put in a bag, and carried out of her house—the house she just died in. Nothing you've heard or seen or read can properly prepare you for that moment. Let's face it: you may have thought about one or both of your parents dying, and perhaps you've even contemplated the manner of death: sudden, shocking accident or painful, protracted struggle. It all depends upon the type of person you are and how far you'll allow yourself to go when—and if—you think of the possibilities.)

For the past two weeks he had walked, alone, down by the lake just before dinner. It quickly became part of the new routine and, for whatever reason, was the only time each day he felt comfortable leaving the house even for a few minutes. Late August, just as dusk was descending, the insects doing their dance with death on the surface of the water. Quiet: the place he had come to swim and fish all throughout his childhood.

Childhood's over, he didn't think, because he had long since dispensed with clichéd ways of thinking. Worse, he had accepted the transition out of childhood some time before. Do we become adults when we earn the right to vote? Or drink? When we first have sex? When we move away from home? When we graduate college? Get our first job? Get married? Have kids? Lose our parents? Decide, for whatever reason, that we have put childish things behind in both the practical and stereotypical sense? None of these for some people; any or all of them for others.

He had thought about his life, and his mother's life long before she first got sick. But being obliged to confront the end of her life concentrated a certain set of scenarios: what her illness was going to do to her; what he was going to do for her; what her death was going to do to him; what he was going to do for himself. These last weeks he had walked, alone, at dusk and occasionally—like now—later at night. In the dark and quiet, alone, he always found some measure of peace.

On the shore of the wide world I stand alone and think.

He stood, alone and afraid. He talked to himself and the water responded in its silent way. He looked down and was once again confronted by the sight he always saw, but still had no answers for. Once again, the scrutiny of his own face, staring back at him, demanded answers he could not provide. He suddenly entertained a curious compulsion to jump into the lake, fully clothed. To swim; to disappear—if even for a moment—under the warm, waiting water. He stood still, unable to decide, unable to look away from his own eyes.

He looked upward at the uncommunicative sky and remembered what he had once read, ages ago: that the light from some dead stars, once it actually reached the earth, was millions of years old. At that moment, this seemed to signify everything awesome and immutable, all that he could grasp, but neither rationalize nor reconcile. All the things there were no answers for.

He thought about his life.

Aftermath

(2002)

i.

I WAKE UP and the first thought I have when I open my eyes is this: *My mother is dead.* Whatever I've been dreaming about or hoping to forget while my eyes were closed returns as consciousness clears upon waking. It's the first thought, a rhetorical question, an assertion, a mantra.

You did it, I think.

At least, I know, the hard part is over.

Now, I hope, all I need to do is somehow go about the business of living.

The worst is over; the worst is only beginning. It will continue this way, I understand, until it is no longer this way.

The hardest part will be the only thing that gets me through: I have the rest of my life to live.

ii.

Making the list. I've only done that one other time, when my engagement ended (it was as mutual as something like that can ever be, so at least there was no obvious victim or villain there). Both times, I dreaded making the calls because I didn't want to impose my grief on anyone, particularly the people closest to me. Even knowing that's what they're for. That's what they mean when they say that's what friends are for.

iii.

Obviously you'll deliver the eulogy, my father said. It wasn't a demand, but it wasn't a question. Whatever it was, it was the most meaningful thing anyone has ever said to me.

Yes, I said.

Obviously. Or maybe I just nodded.

Of course I would, and without thinking about it (because nobody who is normal thinks things like this), I understood that I'd been preparing all along for this moment.

iv.

I remember little about the viewings (I know we called my grandparents' wakes but I don't think anyone says that anymore), except for the faces. Just walking into that airless room and seeing my history to that point standing in front of me. Many of the people I loved best in the world willing me to find my way through the next moment. These are the things that sustain us, and tell us we've managed—through the fortuitous balance of luck and design—to live a worthwhile life. We absorb that inspiration like air and it carries us along, even if we don't realize we're standing. And we file it away, storing it greedily for the darker days that everyone knows will be waiting in the future, like exits on a highway.

v.

During those last months, the ugly *before* and interminable *after*, I'd mostly been too dejected to drink. And that was fine, this was a good thing; the last thing anyone needs is to pour poison on the smoking embers of distress and isolation. And I *was* isolated, then, and found myself isolated after. Now had arrived; it was *now* now.

With death comes relief. For the one suffering, for the ones witnessing the suffering. But it only begins the ceaseless cycle of grief and mourning. And the memories. It was arduous to imagine those who would have to deal with their parents' old age, infirmity, and the endless hours of dead time, before death. There was never anything good, at any time, about death and dying. The question during this time becomes this: Is there anything good about *living*?

Eventually I began to come around. Old habits, routines, distractions. I knew I was normal when I began doing dumb things. Like drinking. After an experience like this, I developed an allergy for abstention—even the kind that most adults work themselves toward and prepare themselves to embrace (the red meat, the cigars, the drinks, etc.). During a time of duress we might contemplate a serial flirtation with sobriety, or vegetarianism (but not church; never church). After a while we come to our senses, and this is a sign of slow recovery. The last thing anyone needs after watching a loved one die too young is something *else* to be alienated about.

Conversation (2)

(2002)

"Hey, how are you?"

"I'm alive."

"I just wanted to check in…"

"Thank you."

"Do you need anything?"

"I need a lot of things."

"Well…do you want me to come over?"

"No, that's okay."

"Are you sure?"

"Probably."

"Isn't there anything I can bring you?"

"Probably."

"So tell me…"

"I can't."

"Why can't you? I'm your friend."

"I can tell you, I just don't think you should come over."

"Are you sure?"

"Probably."

"Well…what *is* it?"

"I don't want anyone to see me like this."

Affirmation

(2002)

HOW DO YOU get over it?

That's the question an old girlfriend asked me.

Well, you don't, I said, using the same answer another girlfriend had once used with me.

Here's what happened: I woke up for the first two years and the first conscious thought practically every morning was: *My mother is dead.* Almost like a perverse affirmation. It reinforced that she was still with me, obviously: in dreams and in my mind and all the places we visit while we're asleep and the real magic occurs— when we use that part of our brains we don't normally have access to.

If you're lucky the same things that provided comfort and inspiration before still do: art, music, friends, drinks, family, faith in something apart from your own skin. You latch on to whatever you can and eagerly absorb whatever it will give you. This is how you get through.

Solitude

(2013)

ANYONE WHO HAS LOST a parent (or worse, a child) can understand that the loss becomes an indelible line of demarcation: your life before and your life after. It doesn't mean nothing is ever the same or that you can never get past it (everything is the same and you can get past it except for the fact that nothing is ever the same and you can never get past it. You don't want to).

Of course, you don't need to suffer the untimely death of a parent to appreciate that his or her presence—in the ways we can measure and the ones we can never fully fathom—is inextricable from your own. Up to a certain age my mother was my confidante, my confessor, my friend, my *mother*. It's discomfiting to imagine how I might have handled her death if it had happened earlier—not to mention much earlier—in my life.

According to the socially accepted laws of society, I became an adult at eighteen. By my rather more reliable reckoning, I didn't become an individual prepared to wrestle with adult realities until I'd finished graduate school and then spent several crucial years learning new things and unlearning others.

The months from early summer 1995 through late spring 1996 did more than anything else to prepare me for the rest of my life, with and without my mother. Severing an engagement and opting not to enter the PhD program that had accepted me are two decisions that befuddled friends and family, then, and likely perplex some of them, still. During this year I figured out, for the first time, how to take care of myself. I was alone, *really* alone, for the first time, yet I found that I seldom felt lonely. Being on my own—alone with my thoughts, questions, and concerns—provided the space, physical and mental, to unravel the reveries that signaled the kind of person I hoped to become.

Being one's own best friend is dangerous, potentially delusional territory and I knew it. But I found that the more time I spent alone the better I was able to love everyone around me, and my capacity to learn and evolve did not abate. When my mother got sick the first person I talked to was *myself*. If this had happened five or ten years earlier I would have been lost, without a foundation. My mother remained my number-one resource in so many regards, but I was finally equipped to withstand the ordeal I had unwittingly been fortifying myself for. Depending on my mind, my music, and an ability to take care of myself, I managed to get through it. Barely.

Dreams

(2002 to 2013)

EVERY NOW AND THEN my mother visits me. Somehow, she comes back.

She's not a zombie, but she's also not quite herself. It's as though she has outlasted (outsmarted?) the rules of Nature and is simply back in our lives.

This scenario is, of course, only possible in dreams. Because of the curious half-reality of the dream state, the improbable—or, in this case the impossible—can occur simply because *it's a dream.* The ones where I'm vaguely aware—even during the dream—that something is obviously askew are always unsettling, even if the dreams feature my dearly departed pulling a Lazarus, that ultimate miracle. Perhaps it's disconcerting in the same way that the story of Lazarus, like so many stories from the bible, is probably lost in translation.

How can we really describe dreams accurately, honestly? It's as though the metaphors aren't commenting on reality; they *are* reality. It isn't that these scenarios aren't literal enough; they're *too* literal, *too* real.

So how do we all react when we see her?

In the maddening fashion of dreams, we're always joining the action already in progress. So she's just among us, sort of like an unspoken acknowledgement: *Oops, we made a mistake!* (Lucky us.) *She's not dead after all!* (Lucky her.) Naturally, everyone is delighted. Still, we feel a nagging comprehension, suppressed but still unavoidable, that she was dead…she has been *in the ground.*

Somehow this is sensible, but not in that surreal legitimacy of dreams. She's not a ghost or an avenging angel; she's simply around us once again. And she doesn't have much to say (this is the most difficult part). She's always a bit defiant, even distant (who could blame her?), as though she doesn't expect us to understand (who could blame us?). There's never an overriding relief that spills over into uncontainable joy, as there should be (She lives!); it's as though she is, in spite of her good fortune, a bit put out by the struggle. It almost seems as if she resents the lost time and all the turmoil this drama entailed: *I was dead, but now I am alive forever. II have the keys to death and eternity.*

Worse, the more mundane but disturbing dreams where we quarrel, something we did very little of, especially all through the last years of her life. It's typically over something trivial (just like real life), forgettable, which is a relief. Yet, the question then follows: *This is worthy of a dream?*

Worst of all, the dreams where nothing of consequence occurs. Not memories or relived events with alternate endings; just her presence. She's there, among us again. These are the dreams where I awaken with a start, half hopeful and full of unimagined alternatives, only to realize (once again) that waking up brings me back and she's still gone.

Discursion: Worrying

Two things my family became expert at during those last five years: taking care of my mother and worrying. We were authorities; we worried all the time, about everything. The better prepared and dedicated you are, the more you're likely to worry. Because you can't cover every angle or option, no matter how much contingency you've built into each possible scenario.

As she got progressively sicker, the opportunities for discomfort (hers) and failure (ours) expanded at a rate that fed off our fears. So we worried. I've since seen people who've been obliged to care for a spouse or parent by themselves, and I wonder how this burden is not literally debilitating.

Perhaps not surprisingly, as things became increasingly dire toward the end, time slowed down and the options and possibilities narrowed. Eventually the only concern was making her as comfortable as possible. *Let her find peace* was the ceaseless recitation I repeated like a monk those last few weeks.

And myself? You don't ask for peace, you search for it and hope for it (some people pray for it). No one is capable of giving it to you, even—or especially—if you're willing to pay for it.

There are many immutable truths we are fortunate to discover before time runs out, and this is one of them.

The one relief, once it's finally over, is the realization that there's nothing more to worry about. Except for all the other things you have to worry about. I quickly developed an intense (irrational?) fear concerning the death of another loved one. Was this possible? (Of course it was.) Was this likely? (Of course it wasn't.) You suddenly become intolerably (irrationally?) sensitive to the prospect—not to mention the inevitability—of the other parent dying, or your sibling dying. Or (awful, irrational) your sibling's children. And then, even if you eventually get a handle on those apprehensions, you still face the disconcerting specter of your own inevitable death.

For a long while there's no respite, because the same things that placate and distract also remind us: friends will get ill and die, pets, friends' pets, friends' families, and so on down the hellish rabbit hole.

My family worried about me. In fairness, I worried about them as well. This is what families do, especially under duress.

My sister worried about me. *He's all by himself,* she thought. *How can he stand it?* I was my own best friend, she knew, and that was good. Mostly she marveled at the peace and perseverance I seemed to have cultivated (when, exactly, *had* that growth occurred? Or had it happened while she was busy building—and worrying about—her own family?). She couldn't help worrying about me and my resolve: where did it come from, and would it possibly last? Could it?

My sister worried about our father. All that he'd seen; what he would have to face, possibly alone, as he faced down old age. She worried about him getting sick, about having to take care of him (and the attendant guilt when she thought: *I can't do this again*). She worried about all the husbands and sons and daughters who had no idea what to expect (they didn't even know what was coming; no one does—even, or especially, the ones who think they do), even the ones who were able to avoid this particular path. If it wasn't this it was something else; nobody escaped some type of ultimate unpleasantness. She worried about herself: even though it was over it was only just beginning. And then she had her husband and her kids to think about. And worry about.

Our father may have been worried or he may have been too busy trying to put one day in front of another. You do that enough times and a week goes by, then a month, then a year. And all that time you might have spent worrying you could have been living. It's enough, sometimes, just to live.

I worried because I knew something neither of them understood: I had by far the easiest burden to carry. I worried for all sorts of reasons about all sorts of things, but mostly I acknowledged how much easier things were for me. My sister had little kids to contend with. On days she couldn't pull it together she had to pull it together. This is, of course, what got her through it. You make enough beds and meals and give enough baths and change enough diapers and suddenly your children are older (so are you) and your grief has abated.

I worried, above all, about my old man, because he had it hardest. Aside from nursing his pain and worrying about his children, he had the responsibility of learning how to survive. It was him, not us, who still had to live in that house. He had to walk past that room, see that bed, use that shower, open that refrigerator, pull into that garage, mow that lawn, open that mailbox, read those letters, write those checks, watch that TV, go to sleep and wake up in the middle of the night not certain—for a second that might last too long—if he was alone.

Whispered Words

(2009)

HOW LONG WILL it take? I didn't ask, because I wanted to make every second count. It would be over quickly enough; it was already happening entirely too soon.

It's okay, I said as I held my dog, flanked by friends and the friendly technicians who split their time between extending or improving lives and facilitating peaceful endings.

"He won't feel any pain," they assured me, and I knew it was true since this wasn't the first time I had found myself in this situation. Another dog, another occasion, and the excruciating decision to restrict pain by hastening death. Another time, at a place all dogs hate to go, perhaps because some part of them suspects that someday the person standing over them at the examination table will be the same one who administers that final injection.

I had already watched another small dog slowly go to sleep, just like they said he would. Barely moving when we carried him in, he snarled once the doctor reached for him: an instinctive gesture or perhaps a final, indignant affirmation (*I am still alive!*) and, as we covered him with kisses and kind words, the calm, considerate doctor reminded us that there would be no pain; it would, in fact, be

quite pleasant. This stuff, he said, putting the needle down, would make our dog—could, in fact, make any of us—feel better than we'd ever felt; this stuff was illegal, and expensive, on the streets.

Another day, different doctor, same drill. My dog's heart was failing him. It was supposed to be a sluggish, gradual decline; the type you can sluggishly, gradually prepare for. But something had happened (I seem to recall words like torn and internal and bleeding) and my dog could scarcely breathe on his own when I brought him in. Seeing him, panting heavily and near panic in his tiny, oxygenated crate was the second-most pitiful sight I've ever endured. I left the room so they could give me the diagnosis: it was dire and I had minutes, not hours, to make a decision. The moment my dog saw me as I rushed back into the room that default setting took over and all my own concerns evaporated.

(*Stay strong*, I didn't need to tell myself, because I'd been here before. I had looked down, yet another time, at another pair of eyes: impossibly lucid and beseeching, charging me to make sense of, or at least assuage, a kind of suffering that can't be conveyed with words. With my mother and without doctors, or answers, to help me help her.)

(And once again I heard that reassuring phrase, or well-meaning mantra, that somehow articulated every hope, fear, and aspiration a moment like this can contain. *It will be okay,* I said, smiling down at those eyes. Eyes I had looked into too many times to count, eyes that told me more about myself than anyone would believe, eyes that, until this moment, I couldn't imagine never being able to look into again.)

Okay.

It gets very quiet while time and place and the guarded feelings that enable us to function all fall away and you concentrate every thought into one simple, implausible objective: *peace.* You think it and you will it and for a moment that might be forever you *become* it in ways you're never able to talk about later, even if you are inclined (and you aren't, especially). You shiver but are calm; you are entirely in the present tense yet you are also somewhere else, somewhere deeper inside that, somehow, connects you to everything else you've ever known.

It will be okay, you whisper, actually believing this because it's not even your own voice you hear. You don't know if this is you, or your mind, or the actualization of that *other* place (you are hazily aware) you have managed to access, understanding it's not anything you can anticipate or comprehend even though you've been preparing for it (you realize, abruptly) as far back as you can remember.

It's okay, you say, and maybe your vision is blurred or your eyes are closed, or probably you're seeing more clearly than ever before, but now you recognize this voice and, as you look down at eyes that can no longer see you, understand, finally, that you're talking to yourself.

Ordinary Angels

i.

MY NEIGHBOR DIED, abruptly, while I was away at college. The girl across the street told me what happened: It was sudden, totally unexpected.

I didn't even know she was sick, I said.

No one did, not even her, she said.

She simply collapsed; alive one second, dead by the time she hit the floor. No warning, no symptoms. It was like she—and her family—got blindsided by a truck called cancer. It had been inside her, everywhere, engulfing her from the inside out.

ii.

After just about everything had been done, every last resort explored and found insufficient, after five years my mother finally knew (this was before the pain, the *real* pain, commenced). Even while we were still lying to her, she ultimately could no longer lie to herself. Her body told her, and her grandchildren—who didn't yet know how to lie—told her. The kids could sense it, and when she saw she was boring her granddaughter, that was a sign. When her granddaughter—the one she helped raise, the one whose diapers she'd changed, the one for whom she could not buy enough toys or treats, the one she secretly (and not so secretly) loved as much as her own children—made it obvious, in ways only very young children can, that grandma was no longer as much *fun,* she knew.

iii.

Generally speaking, illness is cathartic. Even the worst stomach flu is tolerable because we know that however awful it feels, it's temporary. In fact, as the worst symptoms ensue, you can take a curious comfort, knowing it can't get worse. It follows patterns, borders, and you can almost predict the course it will take. Then, as you gradually begin to improve, it becomes slightly intoxicating: the nasal drip that made it hard to swallow and difficult to sleep now congealed and coughed up, expired demons exorcised from your system. Your vitality stumbles back, like an eager baby learning to walk, and eventually, you're yourself again.

With terminal cancer there's no improvement, and each time you confront the worst possible symptoms, more are always on offer, a never-ending supply promising agonies you could not have previously imagined.

iv.

To hear some people tell it, angels are all around us. Lincoln spoke about the better angels of our nature, but these people believe actual angels are guiding our lives, their handiwork resulting in what we can only call miracles.

It's certainly an enchanting notion: our departed loved ones— or unknowable spiritual beings—looking down from heaven, intervening on God's orders, helping us do what we can't do for ourselves.

We see evidence each day of the ways our fellow human beings make concepts like angels, heaven, and even hell seem like the only sensible remedy for the evils we inflict. Even if, guided by angels or their influence over our natures, we established a better way to exist, we would still have inexorable setbacks like illness and death—the sorts of circumstances that practically compel divine exegesis.

v.

Question: What would you have done differently?

Answer: I would have brought in hospice much sooner.

Question: Why didn't you?

Answer: I didn't realize it was an option.

vi.

Listen: for a country that prides itself on doing so many things so well, America doesn't handle dying with any particular aplomb. In fact, we are decidedly inadequate when it comes to confronting death, much less embracing dying as a natural process, an opportunity to heal the living.

For more than five years, my family fought cancer. We faced multiple turning points and uncompromised choices. When we finally realized that hospice was an option—and despite the gratitude we collectively feel, in hindsight—the decision to take that step was far from uncomplicated. It obliged us to acknowledge a reality we could no longer elude: the woman we loved was increasingly close to death, and we could do increasingly little about it.

We brought in hospice. We did the research, made the choices, placed the calls, faced our fears.

The hospice nurse who visited us that first morning was calm and kind as my mother sat in the bedroom unable to control her shaking limbs, looking like a child who had been caught shoplifting. Within minutes, the nurse established a bond with my mother. Within hours, she managed to become all things to everyone involved, talking and listening to the rest of us as we sat around the kitchen table, a benevolent vessel who received—and seemingly resolved—every concern about medications, how to communicate (with my mother, amongst ourselves), how to navigate the unfathomable process of helping someone die with as much dignity and peace as possible.

Our nurse was the only hospice worker who visited us—for some families, a hospice doctor will visit as well, or a social worker, or a home health aide—and she was a miracle worker. She managed to console and reassure us at a time when we needed it most: *You are doing right by your mother; you are bringing love and serenity to an impossible situation.* The contrast between her and the overworked, anonymous nurses we'd dealt with to date had a profound, soothing effect. The seemingly simple, heretofore unthinkable access to a consistent, reliable advocate made a difference we could not have articulated only weeks earlier.

That's what they do, I thought. This is what they do, I say now to anyone who will listen. Hospice helps you help yourself: it's that simple, that extraordinary.

Hospice workers are angels of death. They help us see dying as natural; they help us to see it as holy. When we're faced with an impossible situation, we can't afford to rely on angels we're unable to see. No divine miracles are necessary, since beings are amongst us who provide the support, comfort, and grace many of us would pray for.

When you or someone you love is confronting a death that will be neither quick nor painless, these ordinary angels can become the embodiment of what God's envoys usually get credit for. When even the most compassionate doctors and priests are unable to offer more than kind words and empty promises, hospice workers are waiting to step in. And that is as close to a real miracle as we can expect to encounter in this world.

vii.

My mother came into contact with several dozen medical professionals between 1997 and 2002. Her hospice nurse was the only one who came to her funeral. This is what hospice does. This is what hospice is.

Conversation (8)

(2005)

IN A SENSE I got married, after all. I married my old man.

We take trips together, because we like to and also because he doesn't have anyone else to go with. If I didn't go with him he would go by himself, which somehow seems worse than if he didn't go at all. Even though he eats plenty of meals by himself the idea of him eating alone on vacation is almost intolerable.

So we're doing a long weekend at Martha's Vineyard—the island he and Mom always visited—having dinner in a nice restaurant. Our waitress, who is older than me by at least ten years, brings us our drinks and gives me a funny look.

"I hate to do this," she says. "But I know you, right? I mean, I should know who you are?"

I smile and shrug.

"No, I mean…you're someone famous, right?"

"Nope," I laugh. "You've got the wrong guy."

She mistakes my honesty for coyness.

"Come on," she says in a lowered voice. "I should know who you are, shouldn't I?"

"Well, you *should* know me," I say. "But not because I'm famous, because I'm not."

"Come on…" she starts.

"I'm serious."

My old man makes a face at me after she walks away. "What was that all about?"

"Obviously she thinks I'm someone famous."

"Obviously."

"I hate to disappoint her. If I was famous that would solve both our problems."

The waitress still isn't convinced I'm not an actor or a rock star pulling her chain, so she's extra attentive and flirtatious for the rest of the meal. Professional, but hopeful, it seems, that I'll finally come clean.

Later, as we're finishing our coffee, my father shakes his head.

"What?"

"That waitress is closer to *my* age," he says, kidding or flattering himself. "Why is she all over *you*?"

"Because she thinks I'm someone I'm not, unfortunately for her."

"She should be flirting with *me*."

"Well, maybe she would if you weren't still sporting the hardware."

My father looks at me, looks at his wedding band and picks up his coffee. "You might be right," he says.

Without realizing it, the waitress and the person she was certain she knew have just given my father permission to get on with his life.

Conversation (4)

(2009)

It's TUESDAY NIGHT. Pops night. Every Tuesday is Pops night, a decision we made the week after my mother died.

My old man and I walk past the restaurants we walk by almost every week, past the restaurant where I used to work at least three lifetimes ago. In the middle of this plaza they call a towncenter is an ice-skating rink. When the weather is warm, it's a pavilion for concerts. When it's warm and there are no concerts, it becomes an open area for kids of all ages to run around.

I pause and watch the mayhem and my old man indulges me. I have a limitless capacity for being entertained by other peoples' kids. Knowing I'm not responsible for them is liberating, allowing me to live vicariously the way most adults do through musicians and athletes.

A toddler, proudly if unsteadily ambling in front of his parents, pauses and looks up at us.

"Hey little guy!" I say. The little guy squeals with delight and the parents give me that familiar look that conveys appreciation and solidarity. As they move rapidly in the other direction my old man leans in close and says, not for the first time: "Make me one of those."

I smile and nod, not saying what I'm still uncertain he fully realizes.

I'm doing my best.

Conversation (5)

(2004)

HER: "WHAT ABOUT YOU?"

Me: "What *about* me?"

"Do you drink too much?"

"I'm just trying to avoid anything in my life right now that could be considered a cliché."

"But you *do* drink too much."

"Possibly."

"Well, that's kind of a cliché, right?"

"True, but so is sobriety."

"I'm not talking about anything *that* insane, but how about moderation?"

"That's the worst cliché of all!"

"Good point…"

"I reckon I'm in okay shape for the shape I'm not in."

"Well, you have to settle down sometime."

"I don't have to do anything of the sort."

"Do you want children?"

"I don't know…I can't imagine my life without children."

"Then what's the problem?"

"I can't imagine my life *with* children."

"I know. If we didn't need to have jobs to pay the bills we would probably agonize every day over which job to take…"

"Exactly. You just do what you have to do and have faith that it's meant to be, you make it right, one way or the other."

"So all it takes, apparently, is faith."

"Exactly."

"So what do you do when you don't have faith?"

"You get a dog."

Loneliness

(2002)

I CAN HEAR the siren outside my walls, its urgency overwhelming the distracting sounds the TV was designed to provide. If the TV was actually turned on, it would probably welcome the opportunity. I look outside and the evening air is awake, all that stands between the hard ground and the soft snow coming to bury it. And then, another noise: the familiar, forlorn song of a goose, making sure the coast is clear for its companions. In spite of the cold, I step out on my porch to watch the flock fly overhead. Finally, a solitary goose splits the darkening sky into silence and sound, signaling to the family or friends that left it behind. And yet, I know that those calls are actually intended as encouragement for the others; that they always fly in formation, taking turns against the wind.

So what was the story; why was this one seemingly stranded? Was it beseeching the ones it couldn't see, or signaling its furtive rebellion?

I think: you need to stop thinking so much, and shut the door.

Beethoven (2)

(2003)

I KNOW BETTER than to try to sleep, so it's just me and the music. Listening once again to the one person who always pulls me through, no matter what. I can listen to the symphonies or the string quartets anytime, but the sonatas—the *Pathétique*, especially—are appropriate for nights like tonight, nights when no sleep will come. That sublime suffering, the solitude, the sacred requital of this illimitable expression. The music, always the music.

After a while, before I can stop and think about it, I fall asleep. Dreaming:

Beethoven. Not the celebrated facsimile of the consecrated composer (the image that often accompanies this effulgent music) staring down sternly at an adoring audience—the people to whom he had dedicated his great gifts—as the applause he can no longer hear surges through a breathless auditorium, but a frail, confused old man, huddled over a candle, awakened from an uneasy slumber and called into the darkness, again, to wrestle with the terrible, silent voices that fill his head.

What sort of God would suffer a man so great to be stripped of the very faculties that once compelled his creations? That refractory grace: continuing to conceive music, in the *mind*, yet prevented from hearing the sweet crescendo of the final coda. Agonizing over those last movements in the isolation of a lonely hour, perhaps looking to the sky, beseeching supplication, a respite, a return of the courage that once restored him.

A man whose reputed last words were *I shall hear in Heaven*. Proof of God's existence for the faithful; proof of life's capricious, inscrutable fate, for the faithless.

Discussion: Bright Moments

QUESTION: WHAT'S IT all about?

Answer: I don't know.

But I do know a few things.

I know some of the things that make me tick.

Even though I write (for fun, for real, and forever), I would still say that music has always been the central element of my existence. Or the elemental center. Writing is a compulsion, a hobby, a skill, a craft, an obsession, a mystery, and at times a burden. Music simply is. For just about anyone, all you need is an ear (or two); then it can work its magic. But, as many people come to realize, if you approach it with your mind, and your heart, and eventually (inevitably) your soul, it's capable of making you aware of other worlds, it can help you achieve the satisfaction material possessions are intended to inspire, it will help you feel the feelings drugs are designed to approximate. *Et cetera.*

This is what music signifies for me. As a dedicated nonmusician, I use this art as a viable source of empowerment; while it remains first and foremost a very real and easily identifiable source of extreme pleasure, it's also a vehicle, something I use to get someplace else. A stimulus that demands a response, inexorably capable of conjuring up words and concepts (and constructions) such as spirit, soul, God, karma—things that are (rightfully) almost unbearably oblique, or pretentious, or all-too-easily invoked, expedient for folks who ardently need a way to articulate the feeling they either can't quite explain or desperately wish to get in touch with.

(When all else fails—and all else always fails—there is music. When the emotions and awareness start to squeeze their way behind your mind, giving way to those awful times when you wonder how you can possibly find peace or make sense of anything ever again, music is there when you need it most. August 27, 2002, was the first day of the rest of my life. Anyone who has lost a loved one will recall—or half recall—the blur of events that come after, all of which are a blessing in the disguise of distraction. I did a lot of driving: from my father's house to my place, from funeral home to father's place, to the airport to pick up relatives. The sensations would become overwhelming at times, and I struggled through interminable hours when I wasn't even certain what was real or who I was. During one of those episodes I was coming or going somewhere and I hadn't been paying attention to my car stereo, and then I came to my senses, recognizing a song I'd heard hundreds of times: in this crucial moment it broke through that haze like the sun and saved my life. I can't count how many times something similar has happened, though it's possible I never needed music as much as I did on this desperate occasion.)

Here's the bottom line: when I contemplate whatever life has in store for me, or even if I allow myself to entertain the worst-case scenarios regarding what I could have been or might become, as long as my ears work, all will never be lost. In this regard I echo

the letter of Paul to the Corinthians, which is obligatory reading at every wedding: *and though I have the gift of prophecy, and understand all mysteries and all knowledge, and though I have all faith, so that I could remove mountains, but have not love, I am nothing.* I feel that, and I don't know many people who would attempt to contradict such a beautiful, irrefutable sentiment. But I reckon, if everything else was removed from my life, including love, I could find meaning and solace if I still had music. If I'm ever reduced to a bed-bound wreck, so long as I have ears to listen with, I'll never be beyond redemption; I'll always be willing to draw one more breath. Take away my ability to write, speak, see the world, smell the air, drink, eat, or emote, this life will still be worth living if I can hear those sounds.

Which is why I make a request to my friends, family, and the medical establishment: even if I'm someday in that coma and every professional would wager a year's salary that there's no possible way I'm able to register anything, as long as my heart is still beating, please, no matter what else you do, keep the music playing in my presence until I'm cold. Because no matter what you think or whatever you're praying for, as long as I can hear that music I'm already in a better place than wherever you imagine or hope I'm heading toward.

Every Time I Scribble a Thought with Artistic Intent

(2013)

EVERYTHING THAT IS GOOD about me is because of my mother.

I'm fortunate, in a sense, to be the type of person who gets more sentimental about the times I read a certain book or heard a particular album than I ever do about holidays. But I'm still human. I can recall the almost breathless inability to accelerate time and make Christmas arrive more quickly. Or the Halloween costumes, Easter candy, or the great Thanksgiving feasts (and the not-so-great family fights that would sometimes ensue). The holidays, as idealized rites of passage, still resonate, but these occasions are incapable of enhancing or obliterating whatever mood I'm already in. As such, the absence of my mother might feel more acute on holidays, but none of these events have been unduly marred during the past decade.

Surprisingly, even the week that presents a triptych of raw remembrance, comprising her birthday (August 23), and the anniversaries of her death (August 26) and funeral (August 30) have been bearable. These have become prospects for celebration, however somber, and I'm mostly able to channel that grief into gratitude for the times she was around, the time I did get to spend with her. Similarly, Mother's Day is seldom joyful, but it provides an imperative to consider happy events and my relative good fortune—despite what's obviously lacking, now. It also obliges me to behold my family members and friends who have become admirable mothers themselves, and I'm humbled to see my mother alive in the looks they give their children.

And if I'm ever inclined to stop and consider how corny or manufactured these sentiments may be, I console myself with the awareness of how increasingly corny and manufactured holidays in America have become.

...

Any time I need to be reminded that I'm one of the lucky ones, I look at the picture taken of me and my mother the day I was born. The pose is not unique; virtually every child has at least one frameable shot of the post-delivery adoring gaze. Or, every

child fortunate enough to have been born in a hospital (or home) under safe conditions to a mother who welcomes the moment and, most importantly, is prepared for the moments (and days and years) that will follow. I don't need to resort to religion or sociology: I can simply consider the circumstances and the infinitesimal odds that I ever made it from my father to my mother in the first place (if you know what I mean).

Who can't recall asking, on Mother's Day, why there wasn't a *Kid's* Day? The response was always the same: *Every* day is Kid's Day. Most of us who have lived a single hour in the so-called real world have come to register how accurate this tired cliché actually is. Indeed, those of us who were sufficiently well raised didn't need to wait long for this epiphany to occur. A year or two punching the clock, paying bills, cleaning up one's own messes—the literal and especially the figurative ones—and generally attaining that independent status we strove so single-mindedly to attain is impetus enough for reflection. Not merely an appraisal of how impossible it would be to repay the investment made, measured in money, time, affection, and approbation, but a recognition of what was truly at stake: the selflessness your parents displayed, putting in all that effort to enable you to become your own person. The best gift a parent can give (you come to understand) is loving you enough to allow you to not be exactly like them, to encourage you to figure out exactly who you are supposed to become.

. . .

Holidays have not been intolerable, no more than any other day, especially the bad days when I miss my mother most. As a result, I reckon I'm not the only one who has found that my birthday is the single occasion that can never be the same. Inexorable nostalgic pangs, the pull of biological imperatives, or the simple fact that I'm still human has ensured that the annual recognition of my birth day is imbued with sadness and a heavy longing I don't feel any other time. If so, it seems a reasonable trade-off: that deep and uncomplicated connection, along with the longing any child can comprehend, signifies that yet another cliché holds true: absence makes the heart grow fonder.

Every time I scribble a thought with artistic intent I'm inspired by the support my mother offered, going back to the days I was a kid with crayons, coloring outside the lines while listening to *The Nutcracker Suite*. She'll never be forgotten; in fact, she'll never be gone. This is what helps and it's also, at times, what hurts.

...

How do you get over the loss?

That's the question I asked a former girlfriend who lost her father when she was a teenager. "You don't," she said. Hearing these words, you can acknowledge—and appreciate—the sentiment; you can easily empathize with how inconceivable it is to possibly heal from that kind of heartbreak. But it isn't until you experience it that you comprehend the inexplicable ways this reality is an inviolable aspect of our existence: it's worse than you could ever envision, but if you're one of the lucky ones, it's also more redemptory than you might have imagined. Mostly, you accept that a day will seldom pass when you don't think of the one you loved and lost. And more, you wouldn't have it any other way.

Conversation (6)

HE SAID: *OBVIOUSLY you'll deliver the eulogy.*
I said: *Obviously.*

Sanctuary

(2013)

I visited my mother's grave the first several years for the same reason I used to attend church: it was expected, it was meant to make me feel better, it was supposed to signify *something*. I stopped going for the same reasons I ceased attending weekly services. Catharsis by commission most likely satisfies only those who don't realize the game is rigged, spiritually speaking. Or else, they *do* know it's a game and they couldn't imagine it any other way. (It's not the people with genuine faith the faithless have reservations about; it's the folks who find their faith so onerous or insufficient that it causes them to act in ways antithetical to the precepts they purportedly approve.)

The historical intersections of culture and psychology suggest that there can be no archetypal way to grieve, just as there are no ultimate answers for how we might reconcile our place in the world, including the non-place before we're born and wherever we go when we die. But there's certainly a wrong way to grieve and grapple with the transient nature of existence. Anytime we're encouraged—or obligated—to follow a path someone else prescribes (particularly someone who's getting paid for the prescription), it's a shortcut to resolution we can only attain for ourselves.

Cemeteries are like churches: created to contemplate people not accessible to those still living. They serve as memorials, affording an opportunity to ponder this world and reconcile our place in it.

I've been to the cemetery, and I don't mind going to the cemetery. From a purely aesthetic perspective it's a lovingly constructed memento for departed souls: names and ages and years connected by what all of us ultimately have in common. The cemetery is where my mother's body rests. Anyplace else I go is where she lived, where she still exists. Wherever I go, she accompanies me.

But sometimes this isn't enough.

So I return to the lake by my father's house. The house I grew up in; the house where my mother helped raise me; the house where we helped her die. The lake where I once caught sunfish; where I swam and drank my first beers. The lake where I skinny-dipped with the girl across the street, not knowing what I'd do without clothes on dry land. The same lake I walked around during those last two weeks, my own routine once the August sun began its slow descent and most families sat down to dinner. The only place I was ever alone those last two weeks: a respite from crowded and uncomfortable thoughts; a retreat from the inevitable rituals of adulthood. The same lake where my father and I ended up, later that final night, after it was over and my sister had returned to her family. The lake we silently circled, not saying much, not needing to do anything other than *exist*.

This is where I go. I return to this lake. It is my church, my sanctified place for reflection. The water flows and recedes, feeding and restoring itself. The trees surround the water, their leaves emblems of Nature's enduring procession. The sky stares down impassively to see its ancient face reflecting up. At night the stars strain toward the earth, fulfilling their preordained purpose.

Conversation (7)

(2013)

HOW DO YOU get over it?
>   That's the question I asked a former girlfriend.
>   *You don't,* she said.

· · ·

How do you get over it?
>   That's the question another girlfriend asked me.
>   *You don't,* I said.

· · ·

You never stop feeling the loss, and you can't forget what you saw
or what you'll never get back. And you also never lose the things
you had, the things you loved. That's the trade-off. The more it
hurts, the more you appreciate how much that person meant to
you. That grief is the best gift they could give you. Loving them
and keeping them alive inside you is the best gift you can give
them. That's the trade-off. This is never enough and yet, somehow, it's more than enough.

· · ·

How do you get over it?
>   That's the question I asked myself.

You don't.

As soon as you figure this out, you're free. Free to put the pain and the fear behind you and move on to the things you're still alive to achieve. *I'm going to write* myself through this, I said. *I'm going to live my way through this.*

And one day it makes sense when you understand the question shouldn't be how you get over it but how *could* you get over it? You don't. You don't want to. It makes you who you are.

Epilogue: Concordance

Be thou, Spirit fierce,
My spirit! Be thou me, impetuous one!

HE STANDS ALONE by the lake, thinking about all he had seen, about what had happened, and what was going to happen.

You can't go home again, the saying goes.

Of course you can: all you have to do is never leave. Or: leaving it behind doesn't mean it leaves you. And certainly he can't be the only grown child (he thinks) who returns often—in dreams, in memories, and, of course, in his mind: earnestly, often—to the old streets he came to outgrow the way we outgrow games and bikes and friends and exchange them for jobs and cars and coworkers. Home is where you make it (he knows) but it is also what makes you.

Drive my dead thoughts over the universe,
Like wither'd leaves, to quicken a new birth;
And, by the incantation of this verse,
Scatter, as from an unextinguish'd hearth
Ashes and sparks, my words among mankind!

He hears all the voices from his life: his own, his mother's, family, friends, the old ghosts, the things he has read and listened to, and, as always, the one he received as much as discerned; the one that awakened him in the middle of the night, urging him (sometimes gently, sometimes sternly) to stay awake, to stay *alive;* the one he had, at times, been afraid to fully understand or embrace; the one he could acknowledge, at last, he should be afraid if he could no longer hear.

He had felt the despair of loss, experienced the ambivalence of isolation, seethed at the injustice of the dispossessed, cultivated a faith he could declare and, above all, longed for peace. Finally, he could appreciate that his peace lay in having a purpose, in finding ways to accomplish the work that needed to be done—for his sake and for the sake of the ones who never had the chance, or a voice. Silence, he knew, was death, defeat. The voices spoke to him—and through him—reminding him that he was not alone. He would never be alone.

> *Be through my lips to unawaken'd earth*
> *The trumpet of a prophecy! O Wind,*
> *If Winter comes, can Spring be far behind?*

He thinks about his life.

Silently he stands, the same child who had once looked up at the stars, scattered like bread crumbs in the dark air, wondering if they really led to a kingdom beyond the clouds.

As always, he thinks about his family, his friends, all the heroes who had created the art that made life more worth living, the places and feelings that comprised all the pain and profundity of existence. All the questions that belonged without answers: all of this was inside. So as long as he lived, and made himself remember, they never ceased to be.

He looks out on the water, at his face, which reflects up into the evening, looking down and seeing the world in itself.

Then the mirror implodes as he walks forward, leaving his shirt and shoes on shore. He strides into the dark, warm water, making his way toward the middle of the lake and diving deep, not stopping until his hands touch the bottom, gripping the cold marrow of murky mud.

Moments later he emerges, sucking in the air as though he had never tasted life before, as though he were breathing for the first time.

Acknowledgments

FOREMOST, WITHOUT MY family this project would not be possible. Jack Murphy, I owe you illimitable respect for being a man I can respect. Thank you for being my father, my friend, and the man I've always been able to count on, emulate, and enjoy life with. Janine, thank you for all the things only a big sister can do, and for looking out for me from the day I was born. Thanks also for marrying Scott, a man I'm proud to call my brother, and giving birth to Madeleine and Anthony, who make their uncle feel happy, proud, and old every day. Love to my aunts, uncles, and cousins, especially Susan Trombley and Pat Mastandrea Saunders, who did right by my mother and helped carry our weight. Unceasing resolution to John and Mary Murphy and Martin and Susan Mastandrea, without whom this cast of characters does not exist.

Top billing goes to my extraordinary editor, Lydia Bird. This memoir has been influenced and aided by many people, but its biggest blessing has been your involvement. In addition to your proficiency and unerring instincts, you quickly became the guardian angel of *Please Talk,* and without you it would have turned out quite differently—and not for the better.

Two friends rise above the ranks and warrant my everlasting gratitude. Beth Wolfe: my little sister, confidant and *consigliere*, my deepest affection for debts I can never repay (and also for marrying Jimmy Norton and bringing Ruby into the world!). Mark Seferian, oldest friend and ideal reader: bless your beautiful heart for being there and always believing.

Thanks to April Eberhardt, self-described "literary change agent," for blazing trails and providing crucial encouragement early on. Also to author, professor, and friend Steve Goodwin, for offering invaluable guidance since 1989.

Praise now to some formative influences. John Taliaferro, who encouraged me to keep my first journal, and tolerated my initial attempts at fiction. Salutations to Mrs. Katz and Mrs. Halfmann, who inculcated a facility for the lost art of grammar—or at least an appreciation of its messy mechanics. Greg Nelson, my first creative-writing teacher, who always had a kind word and calm vibe. Iain Caddell (RIP) for being himself, and Chuck Cascio for instilling an eye for detail alongside intolerance for lazy mistakes. Particular cheers extended to Devon Hodges, my graduate-school advisor, mentor, and professor, who, improbably, gave me the best advice about circumventing a career in academia.

Highest gratitude to some of the teachers I never met, but cherish like relatives. Stephen King, who made me aspire to be a writer, and Lloyd Alexander (RIP), who guided me down an indelible path. My heavily-burdened bookshelves sing a song of impact and inspiration; Poe, Melville, O'Connor, Kundera, Vonnegut, and Amis stand out among their brethren. The great Russians cannot be ignored: Chekhov for the miracles he made seem natural, Dostoyevsky (duh), and, obviously, Tolstoy for reminding us what nobody else should attempt to do. John Keats, Percy

Bysshe Shelley, Czeslaw Milosz, and Charles Bukowski, above all other poets, for giving me Faith with a capital F.

Special thanks to Keats for pages 227 and 228 ("When I have Fears that I may Cease to Be"); Shelley for pages 277 and 278 ("Ode to the West Wind"), and Milosz for pages ix ("On Angels") and 83 ("Return to Kraków in 1880"). Also Ralph Ellison for page 10 *(Invisible Man)*, William Blake for pages 37 ("The Tyger") and 89 ("The Everlasting Gospel"), and Robert Hayden for page 70 ("Those Winter Sundays").

And now the music, without which I'd be nothing. A short list of saviors: Bach, Beethoven, and Mozart; the Beatles, Ian Anderson, Neil Peart, Peter Gabriel, and Pete Townshend. Jim Morrison, whose example suggested things to do and, more importantly, things *not* to do. All-time heroes Charles Mingus, John Coltrane, and Rahsaan Roland Kirk, for scoffing at adversity and making the kind of magic anyone can believe in; Eric Dolphy and Booker Little, for their courage in an unkind world. Hat-tips to Miles, Monk, Sun Ra, and Zorn, for inventing new realities and forever flouting conformity. Bob Marley, we remain unworthy of the light you left us all. Led Zeppelin, for keeping me forever In The Light. Jimi Hendrix, anything beyond this world is a luxury, because you are all the proof I need regarding angels, souls, and salvation. Entirely too many others to list.

Credit and kudos to the doctors who have helped my family and me, including Dr. Martha Kendall and Dr. Milly Shah: thank you both for proving that expertise and empathy can coexist in modern medicine. Dr. Jim Boyer, Dr. John Marshall, and especially Katie, from hospice. Maggie Callanan, author and retired hospice nurse, I salute you for being a godmother of sorts to my literary ambitions, and for your kind words of wisdom during the final days of my mother's life. I'd also like, formally and humbly, to acknowledge this world's overlooked nurses, all of whom deserve more credit and esteem for the critical tasks they perform.

My band of brothers: Matthew Canada, trusted reader, partner in crime, and fellow bourbon enthusiast; Shieldsy and Ace, the rock and scissors to my paper; Tony James and Daniel Webb, two of the most loyal and generous gentlemen on the planet; Drew Floyd, Tom Hoyler, Scott Hughes, and Ben Mayrides, my boys from Epsilon; Matt Gravett and Marc Cascio, the instigators of too many good memories to recount; Jerry Erickson, Chris Holland, and Jason Herskowitz, for ably representing Old School; Bruce Studler and Gene McCallister, wherever you both may be, for so many professional and personal lessons learned; Jamie Casello, for being "that guy", always eager to walk through the fire with a wink and a pint; A.J. Hernandez, who has never wavered as a fan or a friend; Charles Salzberg, for the wisdom and generosity; Steve "The Flave" Flavin and Rich "The Sap" Sapio, for helping me defy quiet desperation; Jon Phillips, for the perspicacity and reinforcement; Mark Hanlon, for demonstrating an allegiance and solidarity that defy words; and finally Jamey Barlow, best bud and brewmaster, and the dude who encouraged (and/or cajoled) me to begin blogging.

Thanks, also, to James Shell and Christine Franca, for the time and attention you bestowed, and to the Neuner clan for being the family across the street—neighbors and friends before, during, and after the events depicted in this book. A shout-out to Steve Case and Ted Leonsis for helping create a company—and culture—I never knew I needed until I was lucky enough to find it; Gary Shapiro, for embracing innovation and leading others, by example; Steve Koenig, a great boss and better friend; my three amigos, Tom, Karen, and Lee; and Paul Misencik, for the A/V assistance and being a rock star in the game called life. Indescribable adoration for my comrades at Web Strategies: the indefatigable Beth Jackson Bates, her inimitable husband Mark, and the ever-obliging Mandi Perry. Sincerest admiration to Sarah Zupko and Karen Zarker for masterminding *PopMatters,* and allowing me to be part of it since 2006.

Robert E. Simon, you remain an inspiration and all of us Restonians are indebted to your vision.

Special appreciation is happily reserved for Randy and Julene Slusher, whose benevolence, humor, and goodwill sustain me. John and Lisa Santoro (and your extended families), you will never know what role models you've always been for how to act in any situation (bonus points for giving us Riley and Logan). Leroy Brown, you were the best dog I could ever have wished for and you taught me a lot more than I ever taught you (also, RIP Otis, Quinzy, and Holly). A special note of grace offered to Sheri Wassenaar James, who provided an early, valuable lesson about love and loss.

Finally, it all begins and ends with my mother. Linda, Mom, Boo-Boo, Grandma: you were known by many names but all of them meant one word—*love.* I carry you inside me and that is the greatest gift and enduring consolation a son could hope for.

SEAN MURPHY has been publishing fiction, reviews (music, movie, book, food), and essays on the technology industry for almost twenty years. He blogs at bullmurph.com and writes regularly for *PopMatters.* His work has also appeared in the *Village Voice, AlterNet, The Weeklings, Web del Sol,* and *Northern Virginia Magazine.* His next goal is to complete the "pretty good" American novel. Visit him online at seanmurphy.net.

34162113R00180

Made in the USA
Lexington, KY
25 July 2014